THE PUEBLO REVOLT

THE PUEBLO REVOLT

by Robert Silverberg

*Introduction to the Bison Book Edition
by Marc Simmons*

University of Nebraska Press
Lincoln and London

First Bison Book printing: 1994
Most recent printing indicated by the last digit below:
10   9   8   7   6   5   4   3   2   1

Library of Congress Cataloging-in-Publication Data
Silverberg, Robert.
The Pueblo Revolt / by Robert Silverberg; introduction to the Bison Book
edition by Marc Simmons.
p.   cm.
Reprint. Originally published: New York: Weybright and Talley, 1970.
Includes bibliographical references (p.   ) and index.
ISBN 0-8032-9227-9 (pbk.)
1. Pueblo Revolt, 1680. 2. Pueblo Indians—History. I. Title.
E99.P9S56   1994   93-44801
978.9′02—dc20   CIP

Reprinted by arrangement with Agberg Ltd., care of Ralph M. Vicinanza
Ltd.

∞

Introduction

by Marc Simmons

Under a flaming sunrise on August 10, 1680, the Pueblo Indians of the Southwest rose in revolt, launching a massive assault upon the Spanish Kingdom of New Mexico. The event would be referred to by their descendants three centuries later as the "First American Revolution." Before it was over, twenty-one Franciscan missionaries, more than four hundred Spaniards, and an uncounted legion of Indians had perished.

This dramatic episode represented one of the bloodiest defeats ever experienced by Spain in her overseas empire. And, as historians are accustomed to say, it was the first successful battle for independence fought against a European colonial power in what was to become the United States. The Pueblo Revolt, therefore, ought to be regarded as a significant chapter in the story of the American nation. That it seldom has been viewed in that light can be traced perhaps to the public's unfamiliarity with this particular saga, but also to the misassumption that since the revolt was suffered by the Spaniards, it is foreign to our national history and thus can be safely ignored.

Of itself, what befell the Spaniards and Pueblos in 1680 furnishes a stirring tale. The origins of their conflict are discernible as early as 1598 when Don Juan de Oñate first laid the foundations for the New Mexico colony in the upper Rio Grande Valley. He found the Indians, living in multistoried and terraced towns of adobe and rock, to be an intensely religious people, but of such a nature as to prove highly offensive to Spanish sensibilities. Native ritual, for instance, emphasized public dancing, handling of venomous snakes, wearing of painted masks, and the sprinkling of sacred cornmeal. To the medieval thinking of the Spaniards, such things smacked of Devil worship. The missionary friars, moved by single-minded dedication, set about eradicating all aspects of Pueblo ceremonialism. Inasmuch as the Indians had never encountered religious persecution, attacks by the Spanish clergy left them totally bewildered.

In the assault upon Pueblo religion, unrelenting as it was fierce for a period of eight decades, we have for a certainty the chief cause of the great Indian revolt. But there were secondary causes as well that contributed to the final upheaval. Among them were interference in village social life by civil and ecclesiastical officials, forced labor, taxation through payment of annual tribute, and the abuse of native women. In addition, during the period after 1650, drought plus several epidemics of European-introduced disease afflicted the Pueblos, reducing the number of agricultural workers and depleting food reserves.

An accumulation of tensions and grievances finally led the Pueblo people to resort to something that they had never done before—they drew together in a common cause against a common enemy. Heretofore, each village had jealously guarded its independence and on occasion even gone to war with its neighbors. But now under the stresses imposed by outsiders, they put aside differences, dispatched emissaries to the northernmost pueblo of Taos, and in solemn council wove a net of conspiracy, designed to overthrow the Spanish colony and return the land to its former independence.

The Pueblo Revolt of 1680 was as much a stunning success for the Indians as it was a catastrophe for the Spaniards. The native leaders plotted carefully. Then they sent boy runners with messages and knotted calendar cords to the far corners of the province. Down the length of the Rio Grande, and from Pecos pueblo on the east to the far western Hopis in today's Arizona, villagers were welded together in a new-found unity and instructed to rise up simultaneously on the Feast of San Lorenzo, August 10. When the war ax fell, it caught the scattered Spanish settlers and the friars in their isolated mission stations totally unprepared. Their losses, for that time, were considered staggering.

The scores of massacres in the countryside, the ten-day siege of the capital of Santa Fe, and at last the flight of the wretched Spanish survivors downriver to the distant El Paso Valley, where they would begin a twelve-year exile, form the bare outline of the tragic story. The rich and exciting details with which those several phases are clothed can be found in the colonial documents preserved in the archives of Mexico and Spain.

In 1942 Professor Charles Wilson Hackett collected much of that documentary record, saw to its translation, and published the results in a pair of thick volumes, under the title *Revolt of the Pueblo Indians of New Mexico*. Author Robert Silverberg has drawn extensively upon that work, along with collateral materials, to fashion his general overview of the event. His book, *The Pueblo Revolt,* which first appeared in 1970, relates in a lively and engaging manner the unfolding of this startling and little-known chapter in American history.

Exactly ten years after publication of Silverberg's *Pueblo Revolt,* the Indians themselves recalled the event on the occasion of its three hundredth anniversary. In commemoration of the tricentennial, the Pueblos in the summer of 1980 staged a series of observances that included traditional ceremonies and dances, feasts, craft fairs, parades, and even a reenactment by runners carrying knotted cords, as of old, from one village to another. One Indian relay team, cords in hand, loped alongside modern highways and then sped across open desert, covering the old route from the Rio Grande to the Hopi pueblos, high atop their Arizona mesas.

The tricentennial was billed as a reaffirmation of native culture and history, a time to assess anew an ancient legacy of Indian unity. A modern Pueblo leader remembered that several hundred of his people in the revolt period had gone south with the Spaniards and settled next to them at El Paso, so native unity had not been quite that complete. But as the leader remarked, their descendants today, still at El Paso, are almost entirely Mexicanized, having lost their Pueblo language and all but a smattering of native culture.

"If it hadn't been for the revolt, the rest of us would have ended up just like them," he said.

In his astute observation can be found the larger meaning of the Pueblo Revolt. As a result of that long-ago event, the Pueblo people are to this day still easily identifiable as Indians, speaking their several original languages, performing ceremonies the Spaniards failed to stamp out, and producing traditional crafts that in some cases have evolved to rank as fine arts. Clearly the effects of what happened in 1680 are with us even yet.

Contents

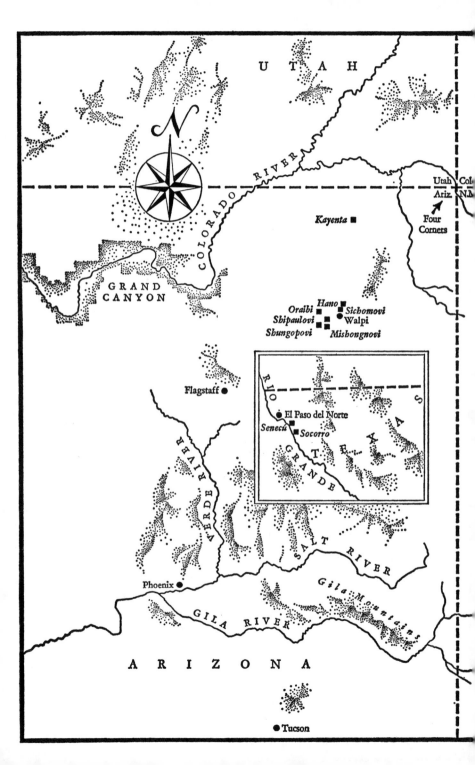

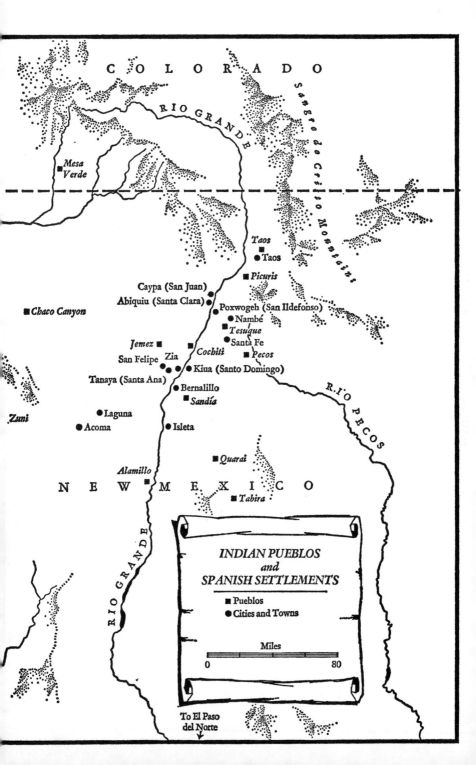

COLORADO

Rio Grande

Sangre de Cristo Mountains

■ *Mesa Verde*

■ *Chaco Canyon*

Zuni

Taos
● Taos

■ *Picuris*

Caypa (San Juan) ●
Abiquiu (Santa Clara) ●

Poxwogeh (San Ildefonso) ●
■ Nambé ●
Tesuque ●
Jemez ■   ■   Santa Fe
San Felipe ● Zia ● *Cochiti* ■ *Pecos*
Tanaya (Santa Ana) ● ● Kiua (Santo Domingo)
● Bernalillo
■ *Sandía*

● Laguna
● Acoma   ● Isleta

Rio Pecos

■ *Quarai*

N   E   W   *Alamillo* ■ M   E   X   I   C   O

■ *Tabira*

Rio Grande

INDIAN PUEBLOS
and
SPANISH SETTLEMENTS
■ Pueblos
● Cities and Towns

Miles
0   80

To El Paso
del Norte

1

People of the Rio Grande

UNDER a fiery desert sun a caravan of Spaniards trekked up out of Mexico to found a colony in the north. The year was 1598; the Jamestown settlement in Virginia and the landing of the Pilgrims in Massachusetts still lay in the future. Most of the territory that one day would be the United States of America was a geographical mystery; explorers had nibbled at its edges, but knew little of its interior. Here, now, came colonists into a province they planned to call New Mexico. Through the cactus-dotted sandy wasteland marched four hundred men, women, and children, led by the royal governor of the new province, Don Juan de Oñate. Eighty-three creaking wagons carried their worldly goods; seven thousand head of cattle, hogs, mules, goats, oxen, sheep, rams, colts, mares, and jackasses plodded beside them; eleven chaplains, all Franciscan friars, looked after their spiritual needs; a handful of helmeted Spanish troops, in armor of metal and leather, protected them from danger.

On April 20 the barren desert at last gave way to a more encouraging sight: groves of willows, a wall of greenery. The colonists had reached the mighty river, the Rio Grande del

Norte, the Great River of the North, which would lead them to their new dominion. Nearly sixty years had passed since Spanish explorers first had gone into the country north of the Rio Grande. They had found many villages of Indians there, peaceful farmers who dwelled in flat-roofed houses of stone plastered with mud, and raised good crops of corn, beans, and squash. So the land was fertile; and perhaps it would yield gold and silver and precious stones as well.

Oñate allowed his people to rest by the river for a week, fishing and cleansing themselves of the dust of their arduous passage through the desert of northern Mexico. Then they headed north again, following the Rio Grande upstream, knowing it would lead them to the *pueblos,* the Indian villages, in the midst of which they expected to found their realm.

On April 30, 1598, not far from the site of the future town of El Paso, the expedition halted in a grove of cottonwood trees while Oñate performed the solemn ceremony of claiming New Mexico for Spain. One of the chaplains held high a cross; an aide handed the governor a carefully prepared legal document to read; a royal official recorded every word of the rite. In the name of God and King Philip II, Oñate formally took possession "once, twice, and thrice" of the province, "including the mountains, rivers, valleys, meadows, pastures, and waters." On behalf of his king, the governor also claimed "all the other lands, pueblos, cities, towns, castles, fortified and unfortified houses" that might already exist in New Mexico, together with all mineral wealth, pastures, fisheries, and other natural resources. In addition Spain, represented by Oñate, declared that she now held authority over "the native Indians in each and every one of the provinces [of New Mexico], with civil and criminal jurisdiction, power of life and death, over high and low, from the leaves of the trees in the forests to the stones and sands of the river, and from the stone and sands of the river to the leaves in the forests."

With this impressive-sounding formula Don Juan de Oñate served notice that Spain was adding another vast tract to her already immense empire in the New World. Columbus had shown the way to the West Indies; the Spaniards had spread from there to Central America and the northern coast of South America; Cortés had given them Mexico, Pizarro had conquered golden Peru. By the middle of the sixteenth century much of the Western Hemisphere had been sliced into Spanish provinces, and Spanish settlements were sprouting everywhere. So many Spaniards had left home in search of the treasures of the Americas that the motherland was nearly depopulated; it was a place now of women and old men.

For Spain it was a cruel harvest, not only of gold and gems but of the bodies and souls of men. The Indians who happened to occupy the lands the *conquistadores* took were treated with chilling inhumanity. They were converted to Christianity, by force if necessary, and turned into slaves; those who would not accept the gospels of the meek Jesus or who would not toil on the plantations and in the mines of the Spaniards were slaughtered like beasts. The gods and ceremonies the Indians cherished were forbidden. Indian chieftains of unusual nobility or intelligence were put to death as potential troublemakers. Terror became a routine instrument of Spanish policy. Whole tribes died out, shattered by Spanish ferocity and by the diseases the Spaniards brought. The holocaust took millions of lives; the martyrdom of the Indians at the hands of Spain was one of history's darkest episodes.

On that day in the spring of 1598 when Oñate pronounced the words by which Spain claimed authority over them, the

Indians of the New Mexico pueblos were unaware that they had ceased to be their own masters. There were about twenty thousand of them, living in sixty or seventy villages spread out along a 350-mile stretch of the Rio Grande Valley. Each village was an independent unit of, at most, a few thousand people; there was no political unity, or even a single language common to the entire region, although much the same way of life prevailed everywhere. Several times in the past the Spaniards had attempted to plant colonies among them, but these attempts had come to nothing. The Indians had already learned something of the Spanish capacity for bloodshed and of the Spanish desire to replace all Indian religions with their own, yet they had no reason to regard themselves as being endangered by these occasional white-skinned visitors. When Oñate finally appeared among them, a few months after the ceremony near El Paso, they greeted him amiably, not realizing that nothing would be the same for them again.

For this time the Spaniards stayed. The pueblo country was incorporated into the empire of Spain. Spanish troops patrolled the valley; a Spanish governor imposed Spanish law; Spanish priests taught the Indians about the Spanish god. The Indians of New Mexico were spared the worst brutalities of Peru and Mexico and the West Indies, but they suffered all the same, toiling to build churches and houses for the invader, working as slaves in his fields, meeting death when they spoke out against his commands.

So it went for eighty-two years. In 1680, though, came an extraordinary event: the placid, gentle Pueblo Indians rose up against their oppressors and drove them from the land. A carefully organized conspiracy erupted into a sudden violent attack in every part of the province. Hundreds of Spaniards were slain, and the others, stunned and panicky, fled into Mexico. Within a few weeks an entire province of the Spanish overseas empire was swept clean of the hated conquerors. And for twelve years thereafter the Pueblos kept the Spaniards at bay, defeating all efforts to deprive them again of their independence.

In the end, of course, the Indians lost the struggle and came under European rule again. In the end the Indians always lost. But it is remarkable enough that the Pueblos were able to throw off their masters' yoke for a dozen years. There is no episode like it in all the long, sad chronicle of the European conquest of the New World. Indians had rebelled against white rule before 1680; Indians would rebel against it after 1680; but only the people of the pueblos ever managed to regain real freedom for an extended period. The Spaniards had smashed the mighty Incas of Peru, themselves fierce conquerors who ruled over thousands of square miles of territory seized from their neighbors. The Spaniards had broken the bloodthirsty Aztecs of Mexico, also famed in their native country as invincible warriors. But the docile, mild-mannered Pueblo folk, striking in unexpected fury, achieved what none of the other victims of Spain could manage. Other Indians, before and after, offered stubborn resistance to the white-skinned invaders, and were subdued only after long and bitter wars of pacification. But only the Pueblo Indians, after having been conquered and subjected to alien rule for nearly a century, succeeded in driving the white men out.

The story is worth a close look. It stands out as unique in the annals of a tragic people who lost an entire hemisphere, a people who live on as strangers in their native land.

For the American Indian, the story begins fifteen or twenty or thirty thousand years ago, when the first bands of hunters came into North America, entering a continent where no human beings had ever lived. They came out of Asia, anthropologists believe, crossing the 56-mile-wide Bering Strait between Siberia and Alaska, and wandering down through Canada and the United States into Central and South America. Archaeological evidence indicates that they had traveled all the way to Cape Horn, at the southernmost tip of the Americas, by 8000 B.C.

These first comers knew nothing of farming, and lived by killing the giant beasts that then roamed the Americas. In the southwestern United States they hunted mastodons and mammoths, camels, bison, horses—a whole horde of animals that later became extinct in the New World. They varied their diet, perhaps, by gathering wild berries and roots, but they had no fields, no farms, no villages. They were nomads, drifting where the game went, killing and roasting and eating, then moving on.

By 6000 B.C., perhaps even earlier, the Southwest was occupied by a culture of foragers and food-gatherers known as the Cochise people, because the first traces of their existence were unearthed near the town of Cochise, Arizona, in 1926. The big beasts had died out; the Cochise folk hunted rabbits, prairie dogs, and birds, and collected seeds, berries, and roots. They learned to build crude shelters for themselves and gave up the nomadic way of life. Eventually they learned how to raise corn—knowledge that came to them, probably, from Mexico.

Corn is a sturdy plant that produces a generous yield of food, and the rate of progress speeds up once a steady food supply is assured. The Cochise people were able to make great strides after they had the bounty of corn, a crop that gave them the leisure to develop new ways of doing things. By about 1000 B.C. they had a fairly advanced agricultural society. Occupying much of southern Arizona and New

Mexico, they lived in small villages near their fields. They mastered the art of basketry, using the tough fibers of such desert plants as the yucca, and made sandals and mats and nets for themselves. They dug shallow pits for houses, roofing them over with twigs and small branches. About 300 B.C. they added another valuable technological skill: pottery-making. Water-tight vessels of clay allowed the Cochise folk to cook their food more easily, to carry water from great distances, to store surplus corn efficiently.

The Cochise culture was succeeded by two daughter cultures, known to archaeologists as the Mogollon and Hohokam people. The Mogollon lived in the mountains of New Mexico and southeastern Arizona; the Hohokam lived to the west, in the Arizona desert. During the first thousand years of the Christian era these closely related farming folk steadily expanded the core of knowledge they had inherited from their Cochise ancestors, building ever larger villages, becoming constantly more adept at agriculture, even—among the Hohokam—constructing elaborate irrigation canals that brought water many miles from rivers to their fields.

The Hohokam and the Mogollon were the most advanced Indians in the United States of their time. But they were destined to be outdistanced by neighbors to the north, in the so-called Four Corners country. The people of the north, the future Pueblo Indians, were slower starters, and were still gathering nuts when the Hohokam and the Mogollon were harvesting corn. But they learned quickly, perhaps absorbing some ideas from the farmers of the south, and built a civilization that developed into one of the most interesting Indian cultures of the New World.

The Four Corners country centers on the only point in our nation where four states meet. Arizona, New Mexico, Utah, and Colorado come together at right angles there. It is spec-

tacularly beautiful country: a high plateau marked by mountains, deep gorges, prairies, eroded terraces, steeply rising
mesas. Cliffs of bright red sandstone sparkle in the hard,
clear sunlight. The air is dry, but the region is no desert.
Where the land is high, it is covered with a forest of stumpy
pinyon pines and gnarled junipers; in the lowlands, the gray-
green sagebrush spreads over mile after mile, broken by
clumps of yucca and bear grass.

Here, about twenty centuries ago, came a group of
Indians we call the Basketmakers. They were short, stocky
people, not very different physically from the Pueblo Indians
of today, with light brown skins and coarse black hair.
Possibly they were originally desert-dwellers from Utah or
Nevada; perhaps they drifted up from Hohokam or Mogollon
country in the south. In the Four Corners region they found
what seemed to them like a friendly environment: enough
water to allow them to raise corn and squash, and shallow
caves along the steep canyon walls in which they could take
shelter.

The caves that became their homes were hardly more than
niches, open to the sun and the wind. Where no caves were
handy, they built crude shelters of brush. They planted their
crops in the canyon bottoms below their hillside shelters,
scratching the seeds awkwardly into the ground with sharp
sticks. Wild seeds, roots, bulbs, and nuts supplemented their
diet, and they hunted deer, mountain lion, bear, and smaller
animals, using spears as their weapons, for they had not yet
heard about the bow and arrow. Pottery-making also was
beyond their abilities then, but they were skillful weavers,
using plant fibers to make the baskets that gave them their
modern name, and also trays, bowls, sandals, and other useful things.

By A.D. 450 or 500, the Basketmakers had begun to

abandon the caves and move to open ground, living in small villages of pit-houses. These dwellings were round at first, but later an oval design was favored, and still later a rectangular or square form with rounded corners. The pits were dug two to five feet deep, nine to thirty feet across. Some were plastered with mud or clay; more unusually their walls were lined with slabs of stone, or a combination of slabs and plaster was used. Sturdy roofs made of timber and reeds plastered with mud covered the pits. An entrance passageway was left open in the side wall, and a second opening, in the roof, permitted smoke to escape from the fireplace on the pit floor. The family slept on blankets and crouched on the floor to eat; chairs and beds were unknown. The Basketmakers probably lived and worked outdoors, entering the houses only to sleep or take shelter against bad weather. The dark, smoky, low-roofed pits were hardly comfortable for prolonged periods of occupancy.

Basketmaker culture grew richer and more complex in the sixth and seventh centuries. New varieties of corn were grown, with bigger ears than the earlier kinds. The cultivation of beans, a high-protein food, was another great forward step. Hunting was made easier by the adoption of the bow and arrow, probably borrowed from the Hohokam or Mogollon. The technique of making pottery also found its way to the Four Corners. Two new stone tools appeared: the hammer and the axe. Religious life also evidently became more elaborate. We can only guess, of course, at the beliefs the Basketmakers held, but archaeologists have found a wealth of ceremonial objects in the later Basketmaker villages: odd clay figurines, polished stone disks and cylinders, "medicine bags" containing small objects of probable sacred significance, and so forth. Doubtless the Basketmakers divided

themselves into clans, organized prayer societies, held intri-
cate ritual observances.

The next change was one of architecture. The era of the
pithouses ended; the era of the pueblos began. *Pueblo* is a
Spanish word of many meanings—"town," "village," "race,"
"nation," "populace." In the American Southwest two meanings in particular are used. A pueblo—no capital letter—is
an Indian village, typically with flat-roofed buildings plastered with mud. A Pueblo—capital P—is an inhabitant of
a pueblo. Though the people of the various pueblos differ in
language and, to some extent, in customs, they are similar
enough to be grouped together anthropologically as Pueblos.

The transition from Basketmakers to Pueblos occurred
between A.D. 700 and 900, when the Basketmakers abandoned pit-house life and began building clusters of four-
sided above-ground dwellings, usually linked in rows six to
fourteen rooms long. Sometimes the rows were built in a
curve; occasional villages had L-shaped or U-shaped layouts,
somewhat like those of modern motels with their rows of
adjoining rooms. The walls of the houses consisted of rough
stones embedded in masses of mud, perhaps with a few widely
spaced wooden supports, and a central pole to hold up the
roof. The roofs were made of heavy logs laid from wall to
wall, covered with smaller poles and reeds, and plastered
with mud.

As time passed the Pueblo architects learned how to cut
and shape sandstone with hammers made of harder rock.
Now they could pile slabs of neatly trimmed stone to make
their walls, using mud only as mortar rather than as a major
structural component. It became possible to add a second
story on top of the first. Villages took the form of double-
tiered series of rooms, arranged either in a crescent or a
straight row. Sometimes they were arranged in double rows;

a front row and a rear one, each two stories high. There were never any staircases inside such buildings; the people who lived on the top floor had to climb ladders to the roof and enter through the opening placed there for that purpose. Since the ground-level rooms had no doors, for reasons of safety, those who lived in them also had to climb to the roof and descend through the upper-level rooms to reach their own.

The pit-house did not vanish entirely. Each village continued to use one or more of them—not as a dwelling-place but as a ceremonial building, known as a *kiva*. The kivas were, and still are, both religious houses and social clubs— "a combination of church and pool hall," one anthropologist has called them. In these underground chambers, which followed the layout of the ancient pit-houses of the Basketmakers, the most sacred religious ceremonies of the village were held. At other times the men of the village went there to talk, to relax, to exchange gossip. Women and children were allowed to enter the kiva only by special invitation, and not very often.

Beyond the village area lay the town refuse heap, where everything useless was dumped: broken pottery, worn-out tools, old clothing, corncobs and rabbit bones, ashes, dirt, debris—a treasure trove for future archaeologists. And beyond this were the fields of corn, beans, and squash where the men worked every day. The basic pueblo pattern had been born. Now the pueblos would get bigger, and then even bigger than that, until in a few centuries more they became huge structures of hundreds of rooms, many stories high.

The great years of Pueblo culture spanned the period from A.D. 1050 to 1300. In the Four Corners country, three main centers of Pueblo life emerged: the Mesa Verde area of southwestern Colorado, the Chaco Canyon district of northwestern New Mexico, and the Kayenta region of northeastern Arizona. In outlying areas could be found less advanced groups who shared some the Pueblo traits. In Utah, in southeastern Nevada, even as far away as Texas, Pueblo influence was felt.

Today the ruins of the great Pueblo settlements of this era draw thousands of visitors to the Four Corners each year. At Chaco Canyon, more than a dozen large pueblos lie in a single stretch eight miles long and two miles wide. The grandest of these is Pueblo Bonito, a sprawling D-shaped compound that once covered three acres, contained some eight hundred rooms, and housed as many as twelve hundred people. The straight wall of the D is 518 feet long. A one-story row of rooms runs the length of it; behind lies a great open plaza in which several kivas were sunk, and beyond is the main section of the pueblo, terrace after terrace of rooms that rose in ancient times to a height of five stories. For centuries Pueblo Bonito was the largest apartment house in the world; it was not surpassed until 1882, when the Spanish Flats were built in New York City. (The Spanish Flats are gone, demolished to make way for still bigger buildings. Pueblo Bonito, though long abandoned, remains.)

Construction of Pueblo Bonito began, archaeologists have discovered, about A.D. 900. Section after section was added until by about 1100 it had reached its maximum size. Elsewhere in the canyon other pueblos sprang up, some of them nearly as impressive as Bonito; in its heyday the valley may have had a total population of many thousands. But in the middle of the twelfth century an exodus began. Possibly Chaco Canyon came under attack by tribes of warlike nomads, who drove the Pueblo folk to seek safety elsewhere. Another possibility is a series of devastating droughts. Archaeologists have developed a way of determining the climate of this period through measuring the thickness of the annual growth rings of the trees whose timber was used in pueblo construction: the tree-ring record shows severe drought from 1090 to 1101, and lesser periods of drought in the years that followed. The fields withered; and by the year 1200, the valley was deserted.

In the north, at Mesa Verde, an equally imposing center of Pueblo life sprouted, flourished, and died. In Spanish, *mesa verde* means "green table," and so the land looks—flat mountains covered with thick forests of juniper and pinyon pine, with deep canyons between them. Atop these mesas, these green tables, Basketmakers had settled long ago, and between A.D. 750 and 1100 passed through the cycle of development that led to the pueblo style of above-ground dwellings. Hundreds of small towns were founded, all of them built in open, exposed sites on top of the mesas.

The pueblos built between 1100 and 1200 show a new pattern, with strong, high walls and lofty watchtowers, as though tribes of warriors had begun to raid the region. And about 1200 the Mesa Verde people found it necessary to take an even more drastic defensive step, leaving the mesatops altogther and building the strange and wonderful cliff-houses. These were erected in great high vaults in the sides of cliffs, protected by huge stone overhangs but open to the sun. The cave-like vaults were not deep—it might be no more than 60 or 70 feet from the rim of a cave to its back wall—but they were so high and broad that an entire pueblo could be built in one. Where the vault was high enough, the pueblo might reach a height of three or even four stories, but elsewhere in the cave the buildings might be only a single story high. The rooms were like jail cells: six by eight feet was a common size, and many ceilings were only four or five feet in height. Each cliff-house had an open plaza in front of the dwellings, where the people spent most of their time; kivas, sometimes more than a dozen of them, were located in these plazas, each one painstakingly excavated out of the cave floor.

The cliff-houses of Mesa Verde were inhabited only for a few generations. In one brief century scores of the lofty, romantic dwellings were constructed, and then were abandoned. By A.D. 1300, hardly anyone remained at Mesa Verde. The Pueblo folk headed south and east and west to new lands, new homes. Drought, again, seems to have been the main reason: the tree-ring record shows almost no rain at all for an entire quarter of a century, from 1276 to 1299. Nomad warriors may have added to the troubles of the villagers by cutting them off from their fields and springs.

The same story was enacted at the third of the great Four Corners territories, around Kayenta. It had followed the general cycle of development from pit-houses to pueblos; about the year 1200, many of the Kayenta people migrated southward, and those that remained moved into cliff-houses, which they abandoned by 1300.

Archaeologists have traced the route of the Pueblos as they left the Four Corners. One group went far to the south, to the vicinity of Flagstaff, Arizona, and merged with the old Hohokam. Others drifted into mesa country between Kayenta and Flagstaff. These are the Indians we call the Hopi. In their own language they are the *Hopitu*—"the Peaceful Ones."

The Hopi settled on three rocky Arizona mesas about six hundred feet high, jutting southward into the flat desert like the fingers of a huge hand. The town of Oraibi on Third Mesa is the westernmost Hopi settlement, and probably the oldest. Archaeologists believe it was founded as early as 1150, perhaps by emigrants from Kayenta or Chaco Canyon.

Two other ancient pueblos are on Second Mesa: Shungopovi and Mishongnovi, which were founded about 1250. Unlike Oraibi, these Second Mesa towns are not on their original sites. At first they were located in the foothills at the base of the mesa; they moved to the top of the mesa about 1700. A third pueblo on Second Mesa, Shipaulovi, was settled about 1700 by Indians moving from Shungopovi. The three present First Mesa towns, Walpi, Sichomovi, and Hano, were also built about 1700, though an older Walpi, on a terrace below the town of today, dates from 1300. Other abandoned Hopi pueblos remain on nearby mesas.

While the Hopi towns were being founded, other Pueblos were building big villages several hundred miles to the east. One new colony took root just east of what is now the Arizona-New Mexico border. Many towns were built here, of which six or seven were still inhabited when Spanish explorers discovered them in the middle of the sixteenth century. The people of this district call themselves the *Ashiwi,* but they are known to outsiders as the Zuni. (Most of the names that Americans use for Pueblo tribes or villages are garbled forms coined by the Spaniards; only a few bear any resemblance to what the Indians themselves say.)

East of Zuni another new pueblo was settled at Ácoma about 1300, possibly by refugees from Mesa Verde. The Ácoma pueblo, situated atop a lofty mesa, was an impregnable fortress for centuries. The only access to it was by a steep trail cut in the side of the mesa. Thus the Ácoma people were able to defend themselves quite successfully against enemies, including the first Spanish settlers.

The greatest concentration of Pueblo Indians during the period following the exodus from the Four Corners lay farther to the east, in central New Mexico, along the course of the Rio Grande. A few settlements had been established there in late Basketmaker days, but those villages had been isolated frontier outposts of no importance. Now, suddenly, the majority of the Mesa Verde people, the most advanced Pueblos of the north, arrived. Through the fourteenth, fifteenth, and sixteenth centuries several hundred villages were founded along the Rio Grande. Many of these pueblos were inhabited no more than fifty years; hardly had its people completed it when they abandoned it and began again ten or twenty miles away. It is not easy to account for this restlessness. A Hopi legend, which has its counterpart in stories told in the pueblos of the Rio Grande, says that the wanderings of the Indians were part of a divine plan to purify them. Just as the God of Moses sent the Israelites to wander in the desert before entering the Promised Land, so, too, did the Pueblo gods require their followers to go from place to place before reaching their final abode.

They were forced to learn new construction methods when they built their riverside pueblos. The sandstone of the north, so easily cut into flat slabs, was not available here. In the Rio Grande Valley they had to build with mud, a kind of construction the Spaniards called *adobe,* from the Spanish word *adobar,* meaning "to plaster." They set up frameworks of poles and poured wet mud into them, building up the courses a handful at a time and smoothing and patting it until it was dry. Constant applications of mud made the walls thicker and higher, until they became capable of supporting a roof and the weight of upper stories.

Each town had its own special color, for the hue of the local soil varied, and the walls of the pueblo varied with it. Thus the pueblo of Poxwogeh, renamed San Ildefonso by the Spaniards, took on a pale gray cast; many-storied Taos was a warm tan; Kiua, now called Santo Domingo, had a deep brown color; the now-deserted pueblos of the Piro

Indians, far down the Rio Grande, showed the tint of the pink clay from which they were made; and the abandoned pueblo of Abiquiu on the Chama River was a dusty vermilion tone.

No pueblo looked quite like any other. At Santo Domingo the houses were in long rows separated by streets; at San Ildefonso they formed a big rectangular design framing an enormous plaza; at Taos, terrace rose on terrace to dizzying heights in two buildings facing each other across a stream. The kivas now were of new designs: some were rectangular and some were round, but nearly all were built above the ground like ordinary houses, and at a few of the pueblos the kivas were thrust right into groups of dwellings instead of being set aside.

Pueblo life had changed in many ways since the abandonment of Mesa Verde and the other great stone cities. The changes, though, had been superficial ones. What did it matter if the kivas now were above the ground instead of sunken, or if the villages were built of adobe instead of sandstone? The really important things remained the same. The corn still grew. The gods still watched over the people. The ceremonies still were observed—the ancient rites that brought rain and a good harvest, that kept enemies away, that introduced children to the obligations and responsibilities of adulthood. Fifteen or twenty centuries had passed since the days when the Basketmakers lived in brush shelters and gathered wild nuts for foods. Patiently, in their own time, they had developed a rich, complex civilization. The people were busy and happy. Life was good.

Then strange things happened.

First came a man with black skin, bespangled with jewels, bedecked with feathers and rattles. He talked of other men, white men, who would soon arrive to instruct the Pueblos in religious matters.

The black man was too lordly, too demanding, too arrogant. The Pueblos did not understand him, so they put him to death. The white men came, just as he had promised, and spoke of their god, a god of peace and mercy. The Pueblo folk, who understood peace, listened with interest. But these Spaniards who preached peace practiced war. They stole food, they swaggered through the pueblos like masters, they peered into the kivas without seeming even to realize that they were sacred. And they demanded gold. There was no gold in Pueblo country. The people of the Rio Grande had never used any metal at all, not even bronze or copper or iron. They certainly had no use for the soft, shiny, yellowish metal that the white men prized.

It was not the fault of the Pueblos that they had no gold, but the Spaniards did not seem to understand that. They grew angry, threatened, blustered, put chains on the important men of the tribes. The people come to realize that these Spaniards, for all their talk of a god of mercy and justice, were enemies who must be driven out. There was war; Spaniards died, but many more perished on the Indian side. At last the strangers left, exhausted by their long and fruitless quest for gold.

The Pueblos shrugged and returned to their fields. Season followed season, year followed year—and the white men returned. The Pueblos killed them quickly: it was the simplest thing to do. But then came an army. The white man named Oñate announced that he now ruled all this land in the name of a king who was far away, and in the name of a god with soft eyes and a long beard. It did not seem practical to fight this man. How could farmers with arrows and clubs defeat men in gleaming armor who wielded swords and carried rifles that killed from afar?

So village after village surrendered, and, though some men tried to resist, the land of the Pueblos passed into the hands of the Spaniards. The long tragedy began.

2

The Coming of the Spaniards

In 1528 a company of Spanish adventurers invaded Florida, seeking gold. The project was not a success; troubled by fevers, swamps, heat, and hostile natives, the Spaniards quickly set sail for Mexico, but their five flimsy vessels were scattered by a storm. Four sank and the other was shipwrecked on the coast of Texas, near present-day Galveston. There were four survivors: three Spaniards and a Moorish slave named Esteban. Amazingly, they decided to walk westward across all of Texas, never explored before by a European, in the hope of reaching the Spanish settlements in Mexico; more amazingly, they made it.

Enduring heat, cold, starvation, thirst, and the perils of wild animals and wild Indians, they fought their way through the uncharted land. In 1536, after eight years of hardship in a trackless wilderness, the four stumbled into a Spanish camp in the Mexican province of Sinaloa, and were quickly taken to Mexico City to tell their incredible story to the Spanish viceroy.

During their wanderings, they had heard wondrous stories from the Indians of Texas about large and powerful cities in the west, four and five stories high—the pueblos of New Mexico. The Indians spoke of the wealth of gold that those cities contained; or perhaps the Spaniards merely imagined that they were hearing of gold. The rumor was enough. The Spanish officials in Mexico City immediately began planning a treasure-hunting expedition into the unknown northern land. The viceroy asked an Italian-born Franciscan priest, Fray (friar) Marcos de Niza, to make a preliminary scouting mission; and the black slave Esteban was sent along as guide.

They set forth on March 7, 1539. With Fray Marcos and Esteban were a monk named Fray Onorato (who fell ill almost at once and had to be sent back) and a few Mexican Indians who had learned Spanish and accepted Christianity. A forbidding desert and towering mountains lay ahead; beyond were the fabled cities, said to be seven in number.

Fray Marcos instructed Esteban to go ahead of the main party and make contact with the Indians along the route, winning their friendship and arranging for provisions. The Negro was delighted in his assignment. No longer a lowly slave, he was suddenly an explorer, a pioneer. In high confidence he plunged into the unknown.

The Indians were awed by the blackness of his skin. They had never seen such a man before. Esteban the slave became Esteban the god. He donned feathers and bells, and covered himself with the precious blue-green stones called turquoises that the Indians gave him, and acquired a sacred rattle, which he carried like a royal scepter.

Fray Marcos had told Esteban to send back messengers bearing news of the Seven Cities. If they were plain and poor, Esteban was to send a cross the length of a man's hand. If the cities were large and seemed wealthy, Esteban was to send a cross twice that length. And if the new lands promised to be richer even than Mexico, he was to send back a still larger cross.

On the fourth day after Esteban had gone ahead, the first messenger reached Fray Marcos, carrying a cross as tall as a man. Then the Seven Cities must indeed be places of gold and jewels! Fray Marcos hurried forward. He found even larger crosses set up along the trail. Another messenger appeared, with word from Esteban that the cities were those of a rich and populous kingdom called Cibola.

As he hastened northward, Fray Marcos asked the people of the small Indian villages of northern Mexico what they knew of the Seven Cities of Cibola. They told him of market-places and plazas, of houses and streets. Some of the houses, they said, were ten stories high. He asked if their inhabitants "had wings to mount up" to the highest floors, and the Indians laughed and told him that the people of Cibola used ladders.

The priest crossed what is now the border separating Mexico from Arizona, and journeyed through the Gila low-lands. Friendly Indians accompanied him. Then, in May, there appeared one of the Mexican Indians who had gone forward with Esteban, bringing grim news: Esteban was dead.

The black man had reached one of Cibola's Seven Cities —probably Hawikuh, a pueblo of the Zuni group. Followed by a train of awed Indians who regarded him as a super-natural being, Esteban had presented himself and demanded admittance at Hawikuh, where no man of the Old World had ever been seen. He sent a messenger into the pueblo bearing one of the magic gourd rattles he had acquired along the way. But what was "magic" to the primitive Indians of the border country meant nothing to the people of Hawikuh.

An elder of the pueblo hurled the gourd to the ground and ordered Esteban's messenger out.

Too bold, Esteban insisted on entering the pueblo. Warriors met him and warned him away. Laughing at them, he asked for a tribute of turquoise. Instead they seized him and took away his treasures. They threw him into a house outside the pueblo and kept him under guard, without food.

The wisest men of Hawikuh came to question him. They asked the black man if he had any "brothers." Yes, he said, and they were white. A great many white men, well armed, were on their way "to instruct them in divine matters."

The elders of Hawikuh could not understand how a black man could be the brother of white men, and, having a perfectly good religion of their own, they were in no need of instruction. Furthermore, Esteban had arrived carrying the trinkets of hostile Indian tribes. All these things, wrote a Spanish chronicler a few years later, "made them think that he must be a spy or a guide from some nations that wished to come and conquer them." So when Esteban tried to run away one morning, they killed him and divided his possessions.

Fray Marcos feared to follow his example. He was alone now except for a small Indian escort, and it seemed certain suicide to continue on to Cibola. Timidly he went forward until he came to a hill that gave him a distant view of the city where Esteban had perished. Then after this one glimpse of the promised land, Fray Marcos hurried back to Mexico to make his report to the viceroy.

The city, he wrote, "is situated on a plain at the foot of a round hill, and makes show to be a fair city, and is better seated than any I have seen in these parts. The houses are ... all made of stone with many stories, and flat roofs." He did not actually say he had seen gold in Cibola, but he quoted a native report: "I was told that there is much gold there and the natives make it into vessels and jewels for their ears, and into little blades with which they wipe away their sweat."

Seething with gold-hunger, the Spaniards of Mexico assembled a large expedition on the strength of what Fray Marcos told them: 230 mounted troops, 62 infantrymen, a corps of priests, a thousand Indian servants, 1500 horses, mules, and cattle. The soldiers were armed with swords, daggers, and lances; 27 carried arquebuses, those clumsy ancestors of the rifle, and 19 had crossbows. As commander, the viceroy chose thirty-year-old Francisco Vásquez de Coronado, the governor of the north Mexican province of New Galicia.

Coronado was a handsome Spanish aristocrat, intelligent and ambitious, who had come to Mexico to make his fortune. He had done well so far, having married a beautiful heiress with extensive properties. Lacking that streak of cruelty that marked most of his countrymen, Coronado was unable by nature to commit the atrocities and acts of treachery that had marked the Spanish conquests of Mexico and Peru; by the standards of his time he was noble and just.

He was a magnificent sight as the expedition departed, wearing gilded armor, with two haughty plumes springing from his gleaming helmet. Fray Marcos de Niza rode beside him. They headed an advance party of one hundred that struggled through the mountains and the desert wastes with great effort, reaching Arizona gaunt and weary. Many horses died. Rations ran low.

Turning eastward, the Spaniards came to Hawikuh on July 7, 1540. At a distance it seemed impressive, four stories high, its plastered walls glittering in the sun. But Pedro de Castañeda, one of Coronado's soldiers who wrote an account of the journey, reported that when they got a close look at the pueblo "such were the curses that some hurled at Friar Marcos that I pray God may protect him from them. It is a little unattractive village, looking as if it had been crumpled up all together." Fray Marcos must have shivered with fear as he saw a city of Cibola clearly for the first time. Where was the gold? Where was the splendor? What had he led the expedition into?

With their provisions nearly exhausted by the desert crossing, the Spaniards were more interested at the moment in food than in gold. Coronado sent a party ahead to make peaceful overtures and negotiate for supplies. But the people of the pueblo, who had put Esteban to death the year before, still were uneasy about strangers, and, in fear, drove the Spaniards away with arrows.

Coronado did not wish to begin his career in Cibola with an act of war, but he desperately needed food. He ordered his men to attack. The Pueblo warriors put up a sturdy resistance against the weakened invaders. Guarding well the one entrance to their village, they bombarded the Spaniards with stones from their flat rooftops. Coronado, in his brilliant gilded armor, was an easy target; he was knocked down twice by stones and hit in the foot by an arrow. Within an hour, though, the Indians yielded, and the Spaniards broke into Hawikuh. They made themselves masters of the village and seized its supply of corn.

No gold, no silver. In chagrin, Fray Marcos quickly found an excuse to return to Mexico City. His health had been poor, and he had suffered greatly on the journey across the desert; but perhaps the glares of the *conquistadores* helped induce him to leave. Coronado wrote to the viceroy that Fray Marcos "has not told the truth in a single thing he said." But the friar had not really lied; he had simply been too optimistic.

The Zuni village of Hawikuh was a typical New Mexican pueblo: a huge apartment house of hundreds of small rooms clustered close together. The people were placid, well-behaved, orderly. "There is no drunkenness among them nor wickedness nor sacrifices," Castañeda wrote, "neither do they eat human flesh nor steal, but they are usually at work."

The efficient way the women of Hawikuh ground corn particularly impressed the Spaniards. Coronado wrote to the viceroy in August, "They have the very best arrangement and machinery for grinding that was ever seen. One of these Indian women here will grind as much as four of the Mexicans." The women used sandstone slabs—to which the Spaniards gave an Aztec name, *metate*—as their grinding stones. They milled the corn by grinding it against the metate with a smaller stone called a *mano* (Spanish for "hand"). Castañeda wrote:

> They keep the separate houses where they prepare the food for eating and where they grind the meal, very clean. This is a separate room or closet, where they have a trough with three stones fixed in stiff clay. Three women go in here, each one having a stone, with which one of them breaks the corn, the next grinds it, and the third grinds it again. They take off their shoes, do up their hair, shake their clothes, and cover their heads before they enter the door. A man sits at the door playing on a flute while they grind. They move the stones to the music and sing together. They grind a large quantity at one time, because they make all their bread of meal soaked in warm water, like wafers.

The Zuni of Hawikuh accepted their defeat philosophically and made no further resistance. Coronado's men prowled the pueblo at will, still dreaming of coming upon hidden storerooms piled high with gold and emeralds and rubies. But they found nothing except corn and beans, and were sorely disappointed. Many talked of deserting Coronado and turning back.

Coronado clung to the dream of finding treasure somewhere. When the Indians told him of a province called Tusayan, a few days' journey to the northwest, that had seven villages much like those of Cibola, he decided to investigate. A party of about twenty men set out, commanded by Captain Pedro de Tovar and led by Zuni guides. Tovar and his band found Tusayan to be a group of pueblos inhabited by the Indians known today as the Hopi. They had already heard of the Spanish invasion of Zuni country, and had learned that the Spaniards were very fierce and traveled "on animals which ate people." (The horse had become extinct in the New World thousands of years before, and was unknown to the Indians until the European invaders arrived.)

Under cover of darkness Tovar entered Tusayan and hid below one of the Hopi mesas, under the pueblo of Awatobi. When morning came they were discovered; Hopi warriors armed with bows and wooden clubs came down from village. They drew a line across the trail with sacred corn meal, and quietly told the Spaniards they must not cross it. A parley followed, carried on partly in sign language and partly through a native interpreter; tempers rose, and finally one of the Hopi angrily struck a Spanish horse with his club.

This enraged Friar Juan de Padilla, a priest who had been a soldier when a young man. "Why are we here?" he shouted. The Spaniards roared their battle cry and charged the Hopi with lance and sword, driving them to their pueblo atop the mesa. Soon after, they surrendered, offering gifts of turquoise, corn, firewood, cotton cloth, and the delicious nuts of the pinyon pine.

Tovar inspected Awatobi and found that its people were

much like those of Hawikuh: peaceful farmers, who lived quiet lives in their flat-topped mud-plastered houses. Again, no gold, no silver, no metal of any kind, no precious stones except a few turquoises. The expedition returned to Coronado at Hawikuh. Wishing to know more about Tusayan, he sent out a second party under Don García López de Cárdenas. The chief accomplishment of this group was the discovery of the Colorado River and its mighty gorge, the Grand Canyon.

One day some Indians from the pueblo of Pecos, some two hundred miles to the east, arrived at Hawikuh to see the Spaniards. (Somehow Coronado's men heard the pueblo's name as "Cicuye," and that is how it is recorded in Spanish annals.) The men from Pecos were led by an Indian whom the Spaniards nicknamed Bigotes ("Whiskers") because he wore a long mustache. Pecos wished to show its friendship to the newcomers, Bigotes told Coronado. He offered presents of shields and tanned hides and headpieces, in return for which Coronado gave him glass dishes, some pearls, and little bells. When Bigotes invited the Spaniards to visit his country, Coronado chose an officer named Hernando de Alvarado and sent him with twenty companions to make an eighty-day exploration of the region between Hawikuh and Pecos.

In five days, Alvarado came to a pueblo atop a mesa more than three hundred feet high. The only way up was by a narrow staircase cut into the rock. This was the pueblo of Ácoma, which is still inhabited. According to Castañeda "the village was very strong, because it was up on a rock out of reach, having steep sides in every direction, and so high that it was a very good musket that could throw a ball as high." Led by curiosity, perhaps, the Ácoma people rashly came down from their impregnable fortress to get a close look at the Spaniards; and though they had descended ready to do battle, they quickly decided against it. Instead they made a formal treaty of peace with the Spaniards and offered gifts of turkey, bread, pinyon nuts, cornmeal, and corn.

Alvarado continued eastward into a province he called Tiguex. Here, in the region around the modern city of Albuquerque, there were a dozen pueblos. Because Bigotes was with them, the Spaniards were received hospitably, and Alvarado sent word to Coronado that he should consider spending the winter in one of the Tiguex pueblos. Then Alvarado moved on. Five days east of Tiguex lay Pecos, or Cicuye. Castañeda's account declares that it was "a very strong village four stories high. The people came out from the village with signs of joy to welcome Hernando de Alvarado and their captain [Bigotes], and brought them into town with drums and pipes something like flutes, of which they have a great many. They made many presents of cloth and turquoises, of which there are quantities in that region."

At Pecos the Spaniards met an Indian who was to cause them enormous trouble. He was no Pueblo, but came from the lands to the east; possibly he was a Pawnee. The Spaniards called him Turk, because, says Castañeda, "he looked like one."

Turk told the Spaniards glowing tales of his country, describing the great herds of bison that roamed the plains, and spinning tempting stories of the numerous "pitchers, dishes, and bowls made of gold" used by the nobles of the land. The bison were real, all right, but the gold was a fantasy. The honest Bigotes told Alvarado as much, insisting that Turk was lying. Turk claimed that he had given Bigotes golden bracelets. When Bigotes denied it, Alvarado had him tortured, but still he maintained that he knew nothing of gold or golden bracelets. Alvarado put Bigotes and another important man of Pecos in chains, and took them back to Tiguex as prisoners.

The winter was approaching; heavy snows had begun to fall. Coronado made his winter camp at the pueblo of Puaray, which he called Tiguex, after the name applied to the entire group of pueblos in the central part of the Rio Grande Valley. Moving into the pueblo, Coronado listened with interest to Turk's tales of gold, and heard Bigotes again deny that there was truth in them.

This pueblo of Tiguex or Puaray, near the modern town of Bernalillo, was different from the western pueblos of Zuni and Ácoma in that it was built not of stone covered with plaster but of dried mud shaped and pressed into the form of walls—the kind of construction the Spaniards called adobe. Castañeda observed that "they collect great heaps of thyme and rushes and set them on fire; when the mass is reduced to ashes and charcoal they cast a great quantity of earth and water upon it and mix the whole together. They knead this stuff into round lumps, which they learn to dry and use instead of stone."

Puaray had welcomed the Spaniards amiably enough, but soon there was trouble. Some of Coronado's soldiers behaved in a swaggering, overbearing way, taking clothing and blankets from the Indians. There was friction, and suddenly a revolt. The men of Puaray started a stampede among the Spanish horses and mules, and many of the valuable pack animals were lost. The Spaniards were driven from the pueblo where they had taken up quarters. They fought back, laying siege to Puaray, but it was nearly two months before they broke in again. Cárdenas, the discoverer of the Grand Canyon, gave the Pueblos a taste of customary Spanish tactics: he invited them to surrender, guaranteeing not to harm those who yielded, and then butchered more than a hundred as a warning to the rest.

By the spring of 1541 the villages of the Tiguex area were under Coronado's control again. The Spaniards in New Mexico now were deeply stained with Pueblo blood, which caused long-lasting bitterness.

Turk continued to entertain Coronado with stories of Quivira, the wondrous land of gold and buffalo. Drawn by the golden lure, Coronado set forth in early May, with Turk as his guide. After releasing Bigotes at Pecos, the Spaniards marched eastward into what now is Texas, finding bison by the thousands and nomadic Indians of the plains, but no gold. On and on they went, lost in an immense land with no roads, no landmarks, no boundaries. Another Indian in the party said that Turk was misleading them, that golden Quivira lay to the north, not to the east. So Turk was clapped in chains and the Spaniards went back to Tiguex to begin all over again. But this new venture was another fiasco. Coronado plunged deep into what now is Kansas, on a journey of more than a thousand miles. He found rich black farmland, and bison "as large as anyone could imagine," and fertile groves rich with grapes and mulberries and plums." But no gold.

At length the Spaniards questioned Turk, using torture to loosen his tongue. In Castañeda's words, "He said that the people at Cicuye had asked him to lead them [the Spaniards] off onto the plains and lose them, so that the horses would die when their provisions gave out, and they would be so weak that if they ever returned they could be killed without any trouble. . . . As for the gold, he did not know where there was any of it."

The deceitful Turk was put to death. The despondent Spaniards plodded back to Tiguex, and passed the winter of

1541–42 there. In the spring Coronado decided to return to Mexico. Two Franciscan friars, the warlike Juan de Padilla and another named Luis, asked to remain to convert the natives to Christianity. Coronado left them. Fray Luis went to Pecos, Fray Juan to search for Quivira, and both men met swift martyrdom in their attempts to interfere with Pueblo religious beliefs.

Coronado's return was dismal. He fell from his horse and he was broken in health and spirit by the time he reached Mexico City. The general who had departed in gilded armor came back ill and empty-handed, and got a cold reception from the disappointed viceroy. Coronado's remaining years were few and dark, plagued by lawsuits and bitter accusations.

The scars of his visit were slow to heal among the Pueblo folk. In their two years in New Mexico, the Spaniards had taken the lives of hundreds of Indians, and the sight of their warriors being burned at the stake by Spaniards as a punishment for defending their villages would not quickly be forgotten. Nor would the Indians forget that the Spaniards had repaid hospitality with abuse, had received gifts only to ask for more. The turmoil caused by the Spanish intrusion had resulted in the abandonment of several entire villages in the Tiguex region, and it was years before the Rio Grande pueblos were back to normal. A somber thought remained: to the south, the Pueblo folk now knew, were strange white-skinned men, greedy and ruthless, who had come north for no reason that made any sense to the Indians, and had done great harm. Some day, the Pueblos feared, the cruel strangers might come again.

3

The Spaniards Return

For nearly forty years the country of the Pueblos was at peace, and perhaps the visit of Coronado came to seem to them like nothing more than a bad dream. In Mexico, though, there were still some who sought to add their land to the Spanish domain, and to induce them to accept the teachings of Christ.

In 1581 Fray Agustín Rodríguez gained permission from the Spanish government to enter New Mexico as a missionary. With two other friars, a supporting party of nine soldiers, and sixteen Mexican Indian servants, he traveled up the Rio Grande to Tiguex, visiting Puaray, Coronado's old winter headquarters. The Indians showed no particular fear of this small band of Spaniards, and listened with patience, if little interest, to the friars' attempts to convert them. After a while one of the friars, Juan de Santa Maria, chose to go back to Mexico, and set out alone, against the advice of the others. He never arrived; a later Spanish expedition discovered that he had been murdered en route. The others visited Pecos and the region to the east of it, then swung about westward to Ácoma and Zuni. The friars made no converts anywhere.

The soldiers decided to go back to Mexico, where one of them, a certain Gallegos, wrote a report describing the customs and clothing of the Pueblos:

> Some adorn themselves with painted cotton pieces of cloth three handspans long and two thirds as wide. . . . Over this they wear, fastened at the shoulders, a blanket of the same material, painted with many figures and colors. It reaches to their knees like the clothing of the Mexicans. Some, in fact most of them, wear cotton shirts, hand painted and embroidered, that are very charming. They wear shoes. Below the waist the women wear cotton skirts, colored and embroidered, and above, a blanket of the same material, painted and worked like those used by the men.

Fray Agustín Rodríguez and his companion, Fray Francisco López, remained at Puaray when the soldiers left. Shortly the Indians put them to death, perhaps because they were weary of the friars' religious zeal, perhaps simply to obtain the horses, goats, and trade goods the two missionaries had. In 1582 another expedition went north from Mexico to find out what had happened to Fathers Rodríguez and López and to the missing Fray Juan de Santa Maria. This party numbered sixteen men: one priest, Fray Bernardino Beltrán, one private citizen, Antonio de Espejo, and fourteen soldiers. Espejo, a merchant, was a fugitive from justice in Mexico, having been accused of murdering one of his ranch hands.

Early in 1583 they came to the southernmost group of pueblos, in the vicinity of what is now Socorro, New Mexico. There wére ten villages here, containing, according to Espejo's probably overestimated reckoning, some twelve thousand people. "As we were going through this province," he wrote, "from each pueblo the people came out to receive us, taking us to their pueblos and giving us a great quantity of turkeys, corn, beans, tortillas, and other kinds of bread, which they make with more nicety than the Mexicans." He observed the kivas of these towns—"houses built underground, very well sheltered and closed, with seats of stone against the walls to sit on." The Spaniards, not realizing these were religious centers, thought the kivas were used as places of refuge during cold weather, and spoke of them as *estufas,* "ovens." He also commented on the agricultural techniques of the Indians, noting that some of the fields were irrigated, with a good system of ditches to carry water.

A few days later the Spaniards reached Tiguex and learned of the deaths of Fathers Rodríguez and López. Espejo wrote that the Indians fled, "believing we were going there to punish them because they had killed the friars. . . . We tried to bring them back peacefully, making great efforts to that end, but they refused to return. In their houses we found a large quantity of corn, beans, gourds, many turkeys, and many ores of different colors."

The expedition had achieved its purpose. But curiosity drove Espejo on. Deeming it "a good opportunity for me to serve his Majesty by visiting and discovering those lands so new and remote," he explored the region northeast of Tiguex, discovering dozens of pueblos unvisited by previous Spanish adventurers, and then set out westward in search of rich mines. At the lofty Ácoma pueblo he was received with unusual friendliness. "In our honor they performed a very ceremonious dance," he wrote, "the people coming out in fine array. They performed many juggling feats, some of them very clever, with live snakes." Continuing, the Spaniards entered Zuni country, finding six pueblos and not the seven that Fray Marcos de Niza had heard of long ago. (Today five are in ruins, and the sixth, still inhabited, is known as Zuni.) Here Espejo discovered three Mexican Indians who had been part of Coronado's expedition. Living among the Pueblos since 1540, they had, by 1583, forgotten their native language and barely remembered their own names. They told Espejo of the journeys of Tovar and Cárdenas into Arizona, and passed along rumors of a province there where "the people were clothed and wore bracelets and earrings of gold."

Espejo followed Tovar's route to the Hopi mesas. There was no gold, of course—only gifts of gaily colored cotton blankets. The Hopi, too, told the Spaniards stories of fabulous golden cities somewhere to the west, but after a futile search for the precious metal in central Arizona Espejo and his companions went back to Zuni. Then the merchant, his thirst for discovery still unslaked, returned to the Rio Grande to explore the pueblos north of what is now Santa Fe.

In all, Espejo visited seventy-four pueblos, with a total population that he estimated at several hundred thousand. This was a vastly inflated figure; nevertheless, Espejo did bring back much useful information about these Indians. Nearly everywhere he was able to win the trust of the Pueblo folk, who loaded him with presents and spoke freely of their customs and beliefs. There were only a few incidents of violent collisions of Spaniards and Indians; at one point Espejo found it necessary to set fire to one of the northern villages, and to execute sixteen Indians by strangling, which was, one of his soldiers remarked, "a strange deed for so few people in the midst of so many enemies." Generally, though, it was a peaceful excursion.

Espejo's travels made it clear that the Pueblos did not form a single unified empire, but rather were sharply divided by barriers of language. At the southern end of the Rio Grande Valley the Indians of some nine or ten villages spoke a language that the Spaniard called Piro. To the north lay the dozen Tiguex pueblos, speaking a somewhat similar language called Tiwa. A little farther up the Rio Grande were eight or ten villages speaking a completely different tongue, Keres. The isolated pueblo of Ácoma, fifty miles to the southwest, also used the Keresan language. East of the Keresan group on the Rio Grande were four villages speaking a language called Tano. North of these pueblos were seven or eight villages using a language called Tewa, different from Tano but able to be understood in the Tano-speaking towns. To the east lay Pecos, the easternmost pueblo, where a language called Towa was spoken, unintelligible to Tewas, Tanos, or Keresans. Towa was also spoken by a group of eleven villages west of the Rio Grande, lying beyond the Keresan group. Finally, in the north, the two pueblos of Taos and Picuris spoke the Tiwa language of the Tiguex pueblos, even though the Tewa, Tano, and Keres pueblos lay between them and Tiguex. The Zuni people, far to the west on the future Arizona-New Mexico border, had their own language, and the Hopi folk, still farther westward in Arizona, spoke a tongue entirely different from anything spoken in New Mexico.

This confusion of languages hinted at a deeper division among the Pueblo Indians. Their loyalties, the Spaniards had begun to see, were to their villages and then to the other villages of their linguistic group, not to any widespread Pueblo "nation." In conquering them, then, it might be possible to turn Tewas against Towas, Tanos against Keresans, exploiting rivalries between the subcultures in order to bring the entire region under Spanish control.

The report that Espejo wrote after reaching Mexico encouraged such a conquest. He fanned the hopes of his countrymen that they would find great wealth in the Pueblo land with such passages as this:

The people of all those provinces are large and more vigorous than the Mexicans, and are healthy, for no illness was heard of among them. The women are whiter skinned than the Mexican women. They are an intelligent and well-governed people, with pueblos well formed and houses well arranged, and from what we could understand from them, anything regarding good government they will learn quickly. In the greater part of those provinces there is much game of foot and wing, rabbits, hares, deer, native cows, ducks, geese, cranes, pheasants, and other birds, good mountains with all kinds of trees and rivers and many kinds of fish. In the greater portion of this country carts and wagons can be used; there are very good pastures for cattle, lands suitable for fields and gardens, with or without irrigation, and many rich mines, from which I brought ores to assay and ascertain their quality. . . .

Fertile fields, the promise of gold, a population of thousands of mild-natured Indians ripe for conversion to Christianity—inspired by such temptations, the Spanish government began to think seriously of founding a colony in New Mexico. The process of founding such a colony was a complicated one, however, and many years passed before anything was done. Anyone who regarded himself as qualified to lead a band of settlers into a newly organized Spanish province first had to apply to the authorities in Mexico City, the capital of Spain's empire in North America. The applicant supplied affidavits that demonstrated, at great length, that he was loyal, devout, and reliable, and deserved the honor and opportunity of heading a colony. The officials in Mexico City, after studying these applications for an interminable length of time, would forward the most promising of them to Spain, where they would make their way slowly through the bureaucratic maze in Madrid. (Unless the papers happened to get lost in someone's office, or go down in a shipwreck on the way to Europe, in which case there might be additional delays of months or years before Madrid considered the petition.) Finally, the successful applications reached the personal attention of the King of Spain, who would act on them in his own remarkably unhurried way.

If the king gave his approval, he would grant a *capitulación,* or contractual charter, to the favored applicant. This amounted to a license to exploit a piece of the New World. Under the usual terms of such a contract, the leader of the proposed colony was given the titles of governor and captain-general, with supreme power to rule in the name of the king. He agreed to conquer and develop the new territory entirely at his own expense, reimbursing himself out of whatever profits he could squeeze from his province. He was required to pay one fifth of the colony's profits to the Spanish treasury —the so-called "royal fifth" on which Spain grew wealthy in the sixteenth century.

Scores of adventurers duly applied in Mexico City for the right to colonize New Mexico, sure that the mines of which Espejo had written would repay them for the effort of sub-duing the Indians of the pueblos. Among the applicants was Espejo himself, who proposed to recruit four hundred men —one hundred of them with wives and children—and spend the considerable sum of 100,000 ducats to bring the province under control. But his documents disappeared into the ad-ministrative machinery at Madrid and did not surface again; even though Espejo went in person to Spain to urge his petition along, he got nowhere. Nor did any of his rivals have better luck. One, a certain Juan Bautista de Lomas, managed to get the Spanish viceroy in Mexico City to approve his petition in 1589, but no response, either of approval or rejection, came from Spain, and as late as 1595 Lomas was still trying without success to wring a reply from Madrid.

Meanwhile an unauthorized attempt at colonization had taken place. In July, 1590—seven years after Espejo's return—Gaspar Castaño de Sosa organized a group of 170 men and women and led them from Mexico to the Pueblo country without bothering to seek official approval. Castaño de Sosa was lieutenant governor of the Mexican province of Nuevo León; he thought he had found a loophole in Spanish law permitting any provincial governor to settle lands that had previously been discovered, even if no royal charter had been issued to him to do so. His expedition, which included two brass cannons and a long line of supply carts, took a roundabout route north, making a lengthy detour through Texas, and after months of wandering came, late in December, 1590, to the pueblo of Pecos. The weather was cold and the colonists were tired and hungry; it did not cheer Castaño de Sosa, therefore, to find the warriors of Pecos staring grimly down from the roofs of their village, armed with bows and stone-throwing slingshots.

He attempted to persuade them that his intentions were peaceful. Through a long day of negotiations the people of Pecos remained hostile, and, as night began to fall, Castaño de Sosa decided he would have to fight his way into the village to obtain supplies. There was a brief skirmish, with few casualties on either side, and the Indians yielded. As the Spaniards entered, Castaño de Sosa ordered his people to treat the natives with respect. But, though great care was taken to win their friendship, the Indians remained timid and suspicious, and on the second night they all abandoned the pueblo, fleeing while the Spaniards slept.

The colonists spent five or six days at Pecos, admiring the many-storied buildings, exploring the sixteen kivas, and ransacking the copious supply of corn in the storage vaults. Then they marched westward to the Rio Grande. The inhabitants of the many river pueblos received the Spaniards in a mood of resignation, offering no resistance. At each of twenty-two pueblos in January, 1591, Castaño de Sosa announced that he would henceforth govern this region on behalf of King Philip of Spain, and asked the Indians to swear allegiance to the Spanish crown and to pay homage to Christ. The Indians looked on, baffled, scarcely understanding a word of what was being said, as Castaño de Sosa picked out the leading men of each village and gave them Spanish titles of office to mark their places in his new administration: this man the *gobernador* (governor), this one the *alcalde* (judge), this one the *alguacil* (sheriff), and so on. At every pueblo the Spaniards erected a huge cross with great solemnity and ceremony, and bestowed the name of a saint on the community: San Cristobal, San Marcos, San Lucas, Santo Domingo, and so forth. Through these operations Castaño de Sosa convinced himself that he had transformed the Indians into good Christians and loyal subjects of Spain.

In February he set up his main camp at the pueblo he had renamed Santo Domingo, and in the weeks that followed he resumed his exploration of the countryside, adding another dozen or so pueblos to his list of those that had submitted peacefully. Proudly he sent messengers to Mexico City bearing news of his accomplishment: he had won for Spain a vast new realm, thriving and populous, which he would develop into one of His Majesty's richest possessions. He asked Mexico for more settlers, more soldiers, more supplies.

He was a conscientious governor. Some of his men wanted to turn the Indians into slaves and plunder their gods; but Castaño de Sosa, pointing out that Spanish law prohibited such callous treatment of natives, refused to allow such things. The laws he cited were being ignored almost everywhere else in the empire, and Castaño de Sosa's followers, annoyed by his scrupulousness, plotted to kill him. But he thwarted the conspiracy and continued to insist that the natives be treated with courtesy. Anyone who would not abide by the law, he declared, had better return to Mexico.

In the spring of 1591 Indian messengers brought word that a new party of Spaniards was advancing up the Rio Grande and had come as far north as Tiguex. Thinking these were the reinforcements he had requested from Mexico, Castaño de Sosa hurried joyfully down to greet them—only to find that the newcomers were soldiers, sent by the viceroy to arrest him for entering New Mexico without royal permission. He protested that he had gone in good faith, and explained to them the loophole in the law under which he had acted, but it did him no good: he was under arrest. He yielded and was taken back to Mexico for trial; his colony was disbanded. It took several years for Spanish justice to get around to the case of Castaño de Sosa, but eventually he was found guilty and exiled to China. From exile he appealed the verdict, and was able to have it reversed; by royal command he was to be permitted to return from the Orient and even to resume his rank, this time legally, as governor of New Mexico. But by the time word of this reached China, Castaño de Sosa was dead.

The work of establishing a permanent Spanish base in New Mexico fell to another man: the energetic, dynamic Juan de Oñate, a member of a family that had been prominent in the conquest of Mexico, and one of the five richest men in the Spanish New World. His father had been governor of the Mexican province of New Galicia. His wife was the granddaughter of the famed conquerer Cortés, and the great-granddaughter of Moctezuma, the Aztec king.

In 1595 Oñate applied to the government for the right to colonize New Mexico. He pledged to raise a force of two hundred men at his own expense, and to pay for all the food, livestock, tools, equipment, and other things the colonists would need. The only costs he requested the king to pay were those for the priests who would accompany the expedition. Oñate asked for himself the usual titles of rank, the right to organize civil and military government in his province, and authority to engage in marine trade once he had reached the Pacific Ocean and founded ports there—for the boundaries of New Mexico were considered to stretch westward as far as the sea.

Because of his great prestige and high reputation, Oñate's application sped through the Spanish bureaucracy in record time, and within months the king granted him a royal charter. "Trusting in you and that you will carry out this discovery and pacification in a Christian spirit and with complete loyalty, I appoint you as my governor, captain-general ... and pacifier of the said provinces of New Mexico and those adjacent and neighboring," the king wrote late in 1595. "I command the soldiers, civilians, and servants who may go with you to accept you as their governor and captain-general, to obey and execute what you may order them, including the rewards or sentences that you may impose on them...." And, since there had recently been some outcry in Spain against the harshness with which the *conquistadores* were handling the Indians, the king noted, "You will endeavor to attract the natives with peace, friendship, and good treatment, with which I particularly charge you, and to induce them to hear and accept the holy gospel."

The Spanish viceroy in Mexico City, as chief representative of the king in the New World, stressed the same point in his own orders to Oñate, issued in the spring of 1596.

"Your main purpose shall be in the service of God our Lord, the spreading of His holy Catholic faith," the viceroy wrote. The natives were not to be "compelled to serve against their will," nor were they to be forced to work in mines, which might cause them to run away, depopulating the province— "which is the opposite of what we are trying to do," said the viceroy.

Through most of 1596 Oñate enlisted recruits for his expedition. Attracted by hope of winning wealth and fame in the north, dozens of Spaniards in Mexico signed up, and by the end of the year the roster was full. But during that year there was a change of viceroys in Mexico, and the new viceroy insisted on reexamining all contracts that his predecessor had approved. Oñate had already begun his march northward from Mexico City when word came that the new viceroy, influenced by men jealous of Oñate's privileges, had issued a decree sharply reducing the powers Oñate would have. A bitter political wrangle followed, and at one point the possibility arose that someone else entirely would be awarded the right to govern New Mexico. Not until February, 1598, was everything resolved and Oñate given permission to proceed.

With his 130 families, his thousands of farm animals, his eighty-three wagons, Oñate moved toward New Mexico at the head of a procession four miles long. He traveled in style, bringing a dozen saddles for his personal use, one with blue and gold velvet trappings and silver trimmings, one with trimmings of black velvet, another adorned with green and gold velvet, two decked with ocelot skin. On the baggage carts were supplies of wine, oil, sugar, clothing, nails, tools, surgical instruments, paper, flour, and much more, all paid for by Oñate. For trade with the Indians he had brought glass beads and bangles, French trumpets, clay whistles from

Mexico, knives, scissors, thimbles, combs, hats, flutes, and other such things.

The expedition advanced at a speed of five to ten miles a day. First came mountains, then dusty plains, then a bleak desert, and finally, after two months, the Rio Grande. At the end of April they were at the gateway to New Mexico, the place where El Paso, Texas, now rises, and there, as we have already seen, Oñate performed the ceremony of taking possession of his province. A few days later the Spaniards found a shallow part of the great river where they could cross into their new territory; Oñate gave the fording-place the name of *El Paso del Norte,* "the Northern Pass."

They kept close to the river as they went up into New Mexico. Some of the oxen strayed; a child died; two horses drowned; then they reached an area where the mountains came right down to the river's edge, blocking their path and forcing them to swing away from the river into a baking wasteland where terrible thirst oppressed them. Eventually they came to the river again, and, following it, arrived on June 24 at the southernmost pueblo. The Indians welcomed them with feasts and celebrations, and gave them lodging. The Spaniards responded by staging a sham battle for the entertainment of their hosts, dividing themselves into two groups and displaying their skill in mounted combat. During the show, one Indian approached Oñate and shouted, in Spanish, "Thursday! Friday! Saturday! Sunday!"

The Spaniards were astounded. They begged the Indian to say something else, but he had exhausted his Spanish vocabulary. Where had he learned the words? After long questioning, he pointed to the north and said, "Thomas and Cristóbal." Evidently there were men with Christian names living in an upriver pueblo, perhaps survivors of some earlier expedition.

Oñate hurried up the Rio Grande, into the Tiguex group of pueblos, in search of Thomas and Cristóbal. At Puaray, a pueblo that had had grim experiences with Spaniards since the time of Coronado, the expedition was received in a friendly manner; the Indians had no appetite for trouble. Yes, the people of Puaray said, they knew Thomas and Cristóbal; they lived a little way to the north, in another pueblo; they were men who had come to this region seven years before, with an earlier group of Spaniards, and had settled in the pueblo when the Spaniards went away. In the morning the Indians would lead Oñate to them.

That night Oñate and some of his officers were quartered in a room in the pueblo that had been freshly whitewashed. The next day, though, when the thin whitewash dried, they saw that it covered murals that depicted the murder of the two friars, Agustín Rodríguez and Francisco López, at Puaray in 1581. The Indians had tried to conceal the grisly scenes of martyrdom to avoid trouble with their dangerous guests. Tactfully, Oñate made no reference to the fate of the friars, and as promised the men of Puaray took him to meet Thomas and Cristóbal.

They turned out to be a pair of Christian Indians from Mexico who had been in the service of Castaño de Sosa. When Castaño's colony collapsed, they had remained in New Mexico, moving into the pueblo that the Spaniards had come to know as Santo Domingo and marrying women of the village. Their lives had been happy ones, they said.

Since Thomas and Cristóbal were fluent in Spanish and in the Keres language of Santo Domingo, they were asked to serve as Oñate's interpreters. With their aid, he summoned a council of seven village chiefs, who were said to speak for thirty-four pueblos; on July 7, 1598, he met with these chiefs in the kiva of Santo Domingo and, as Castaño de Sosa had done earlier, invited them to swear allegiance to Spain. Oñate explained who the King of Spain was and pledged that this far off monarch would protect them, through Oñate, against all of their enemies. He told them about Christ, also, and urged them to accept baptism. At the end of the meeting, the seven chiefs uttered what the Spaniards believed was an oath of allegiance to the king and to Oñate; then they knelt and kissed Oñate's hand, and the hand of Father Juan de Escalona, the representative of the church. In this way did Oñate begin his rule over New Mexico, though it is doubtful that the Indian leaders really understood much of what Thomas and Cristóbal had told them, or if they were aware that by their act of submission they had given away their freedom.

As he continued northward along the Rio Grande, Oñate obtained the same sort of submission at every pueblo he visited. On July 11 he came to the pueblo of Caypa, on the west bank of the Rio Grande. He won the allegiance of the people and told them that the name of their village thenceforth would be San Juan. Near it, he decided, he would place his colony's capital, which would be known as San Gabriel.

Construction of San Gabriel began on August 11 with the digging of a ditch to bring water from the river to the town site. On August 23 the Spaniards started to erect a church, and, with the aid of fifteen hundred Indians, they managed to complete the structure by September 7. The following day the first mass was celebrated in the new building, with the heads of all the pueblos on hand to watch the white man's sacred ritual. Oñate informed them that Spanish priests would soon be taking up residence among them to teach them the ways of the Christian religion.

An accident of the weather had made the Indians curious about Christianity. It had been a dry summer along the Rio

Grande, and the corn was drooping in the fields; if rain did not come soon, the harvest would be imperiled. The Indians had begged their gods for mercy, performing the dances that were supposed to bring rain, and yet there was no rain. In their distress they spoke of the problem to two of the Spanish priests, who calmed them and promised to pray to the Christian God for rain. At once the Indians ceased their lamentations, causing one of Oñate's officers to compare them sarcastically to "little children who hush when they are given the things they have cried for." All day and that night and the next day the Indians looked into a sky "as clear as a diamond," searching for rain; and suddenly rain fell in astonishing torrents. The corn was saved, and the Pueblo folk, in awe, told one another that the Spaniards had brought a powerful god indeed.

On September 9, then, the day after the first mass at San Gabriel, Oñate called all the Pueblo chiefs together, swore them once more to allegiance to the Spanish crown, and turned the meeting over to Fray Alonso Martínez, the leader of the priests of the expedition. Fray Alonso asked them if they were willing to accept the religion of Christ. The chiefs conferred, and after a while replied that they desired to know more about Christianity. If they approved of what they heard, they would let themselves be baptized; but if they did not like it, they hoped the Spaniards would not force them to embrace it. This seemed a reasonable attitude in the eyes of Oñate and Fray Alonso. Oñate decreed thereupon that New Mexico was to be divided into seven administrative districts: one covering the Keres-speaking pueblos, one taking in the Tiguex group, one including Ácoma, Zuni, and points west, and so on. Fray Alonzo then named a Franciscan friar to go into each of these districts, alone, and explain the teachings of Christ to its inhabitants.

The political organization of New Mexico followed the same lines. As his personal representative in each district Oñate assigned a Spanish official, with the title of *alcalde mayor,* "high judge." The *alcalde* was to have jurisdiction over all the people of his district, both Indians and Spanish settlers. The pueblos would be allowed a large measure of self-government, although their officers were to be chosen by the *alcalde* in consultation with the district's missionary friar. They would pick a native governor for each pueblo, a lieutenant-governor, a sheriff, and a labor boss; the governor would be assisted in his work by Indian *regidores,* or councilmen, drawn from the wisest and most trustworthy men of the pueblo. A similar governmental structure was to be established for the Spanish villages as they were founded.

Of course, the pueblos already had governments of their own. Every village had six to ten secret societies, each of them usually having its own kiva, its own officials, its own roll of members, and its own special religious responsibilities: one was a rain-making society, one a disease-curing society, one a society of clowns who performed during sacred rituals, et cetera. The leaders of the secret societies would pick the ruler of the pueblo, whom the Spaniards called the *cacique,* meaning "chief." The cacique was the spiritual head of the pueblo, a kind of high priest, chosen for a life term. He was a remote and rather lofty figure in the village, who could not become involved in any quarrels or mix too closely into pueblo politics; he was the only man in the pueblo exempt from work in the fields. The cacique determined the date for performing each religious ritual and presided over the spiritual life of the community. All the most profound decisions of the pueblo were made by the cacique, but lesser matters having to do with day-by-day affairs were handled by others.

The Spaniards were aware of the existence of the caciques,

but did not find them useful for administrative tasks because of their otherworldly nature; therefore the system of governors and sheriffs was imposed on the pueblos. The Indians adapted to this in a simple and practical way, accepting the village government that the Spaniards dictated as an entity separate and subordinate to their existing government. It was the cacique who appointed the governor, naming a new one annually. For the sake of avoiding trouble the Spaniards always went along with the choice. The governor served as the go-between with the Spaniards, receiving and conferring with the Spanish officials who came to the village, relaying their orders and messages to the people, and administering the laws that the Spaniards had decreed. But real authority remained with the cacique. The Spaniards dealt with the governor as though he were the leader of the people, but they realized at least dimly that the governor was merely the spokesman for the cacique. This arrangement has persisted into modern times. Each pueblo still has a cacique, elected for life, and a governor whom the cacique selects for a one-year or two-year term. The governor takes care of such things as granting permits to the tourists who wish to photograph the village, and dealing with state and federal officials when they have business with the pueblo, but more significant affairs remain the responsibility of the cacique.

The missionary friars departed quickly for their remote districts. The task of creating the political organization of the colony proceeded swiftly. No one among the Indians, so far, had questioned Oñate's right to take control of New Mexico. He had been both tactful and firm, and everything had happened so quickly that the Indians scarcely comprehended the change that had come upon their land. Oñate now claimed himself the master of a domain covering 87,000 miles, from El Paso del Norte in the south to the pueblo of

Taos in the north, from Pecos in the east to the Hopi villages in the west. All had gone well.

The time had come now to explore the surrounding region. In winning his province Oñate had incurred immense expenses; he had begun to think of how he was going to recoup his fortunes. In the middle of September he sent a party of sixty men commanded by his nephew, Vicente de Zaldívar, to explore the bison plains east of Pecos. Perhaps, Oñate thought, Zaldívar would find the golden city of Quivira, for which Coronado had searched so fruitlessly; at the very least, he could bring back some young bison to be domesticated and profitably bred by the settlers. Oñate himself intended to go in the opposite direction, into the western part of his province, to search for the mines of which Espejo had written, then to find the coast of the Pacific Ocean, where he hoped to collect pearls. On October 6, 1598, Oñate rode out of his capital to begin his quest for treasure.

4

Spanish New Mexico

OÑATE started by going southeast to search for some reported salines, or salt deposits, beyond the mountains. The salines were indeed there, and promised to be of great value to the fledgling colony. Then he turned westward. On October 27 he reached Ácoma, the mesa-top pueblo. Zutucapan, the cacique of Ácoma, had been the only important Indian leader who had not attended the ceremonies at San Gabriel in September—because, he claimed, the invitation Oñate sent had not been delivered to him. Actually Zutucapan had received the invitation, but had chosen not to go, for he intended to resist the Spanish takeover of his country.

A few days before Oñate's arrival at Ácoma, Zutucapan had delivered a fiery speech, urging his people to attack the Spaniards. At first he won support; however, his son Zutancalpo and a shrewd old leader named Chumpo succeeded in persuading the Ácomans that such a course would be suicidal. The pueblo resolved to give Oñate a warm greeting. Zutucapan, though, along with twelve of his followers, secretly plotted the Spanish governor's death: they would lure Oñate into a kiva and assassinate him.

Fortunately, Oñate shrugged off the invitation to see the fatal kiva, and never realized that anyone in Ácoma opposed him. He presided over the customary ceremony of formal submission to Spain, and moved on to visit Zuni, where he found another rich saline, and again received pledges of loyalty. Next came a tour of the Hopi towns, and more ceremonies of submission. From there Oñate sent a scouting party into central Arizona to look for the mines Espejo had seen. The scouts succeeding in finding them, and came back joyously laden with silver ore. But that was the last good news Oñate had on this journey. He had expected to find the Pacific not far beyond Hopi country, though he had no sound reason for this hope, since the region west of the Colorado River had never been explored by Europeans. Dreaming of pearls, he pushed westward, but by the beginning of December he was still plodding through a miserable wasteland, with the coast nowhere in sight.

Meanwhile, after fifty-four days of exploration east of Pecos, Vicente de Zaldívar had returned to San Gabriel on November 8. He had not found glittering Quivira, nor had he been able to capture a breeding stock of bison; he drove the animals into corrals, but they all "died of rage" within an hour, and he came back with nothing except hides and meat.

Oñate had left Vicente's older brother, twenty-eight-year-old Juan de Zaldívar, in charge of the capital. By previous arrangement, Juan set out to follow Oñate when Vicente returned, and Vicente took over command of the colony's home base. On November 18, Juan de Zaldívar left San Gabriel at the head of a force of thirty soldiers, and on the first of December they arrived at Ácoma. The Indians greeted them pleasantly, and when Zaldívar asked for food, they promised to give him whatever he needed if he would come to the top of the mesa the next morning.

Lulled by this reception, the Spaniards clambered up the narrow trail to the 357-foot-high summit of Ácoma, leaving only four men below to guard the horses. The cacique, Zutucapan, met them smilingly, inviting the Spaniards to enter the town, to go to this house and that one for their provisions. Zaldívar and his men went forward and at once found themselves separated, lost in Ácoma's maze of narrow streets.

Now they were at Zutucapan's mercy, and he did what he had been prevented from doing some weeks before when Oñate had come to Ácoma. At a signal, Zutucapan's followers attacked; the Spaniards were surrounded by hundreds of shouting Indians, wielding lances, bows, wooden clubs. A desperate three-hour hand-to-hand battle ensued. The Spaniards fought furiously, shrugging off terrible wounds as they drove the Indians back with sword and dagger, but one by one they fell. In the midst of the fray was Juan de Zaldívar, refusing to go down, shouting encouragement to his men. Three times he was struck to the ground, but got up each time; when he was hit the fourth time he lay still, and the Ácomans cut him to pieces. Five of his comrades survived. Taking a wild chance, they fought their way to the edge of the mesa and leaped off, preferring a drop of hundreds of feet to the fate the Indians surely would provide.

Miraculously, four of them landed in thick drifts of sand at the base of the mesa, and got up stunned but alive. The other man struck the side of the cliff and died. The men who had been waiting with the horses carried the survivors away before the Indians could give pursuit.

The little band of remaining Spaniards split into three groups. One party hastened back to the capital to bring news of the massacre to Vicente de Zaldívar. Another struck out westward to find Oñate and tell him what had happened. The rest set forth to visit the isolated friars in their lonely missionary outposts, so that they could be warned of possible danger. Would all the pueblos now turn against the Spaniards? Were the "submissions" of the caciques merely pretenses to throw the invaders off guard?

Oñate, still seeking the ocean, listened in dismay to the story, and, calling off his exploring trip at once, marched back to the capital. He arrived on December 21. It was important, he knew, to make an immediate example of Ácoma, lest the other pueblos take up arms as well, and so, after a meeting with his lieutenants and the friars, he proclaimed "war by blood and fire" against the rebellious village. Early in 1599 a punitive force of seventy men, led by Vicente de Zaldívar, marched toward Ácoma.

Sending so many men was a calculated risk, for now San Gabriel itself had few defenders. A rumor spread that the Indians of the nearby pueblo of San Juan were about to attack. Oñate doubled the sentinels and kept fires burning all night; even the women of the colony volunteered to help stand watch. No attack came, however. And at the end of January the first messengers returned with word of what had taken place at Ácoma.

Vicente de Zaldívar had reached the pueblo on January 21. He found the Indians expecting trouble; they danced along the rim of the mesa and screamed their defiance at the Spaniards. When the Ácomans rejected Zaldívar's request that they yield peacefully, he launched his attack. While the main body of the Spanish force noisily started to climb the mesa in front, Zaldívar and eleven picked men stole around back and clawed their way to the top by scaling a rock face that the natives thought was impossible to ascend. Bursting into the midst of the surprised Indians, Zaldívar's little band created such confusion that the rest of the troops were able to get to the summit. A battle lasting three days now began, marked by extraordinary feats of heroism on both sides. The Spaniards brought a pair of cannons into the pueblo and fired into a mass of warriors, killing dozens and driving the rest back in terror. By the third day the pueblo was in flames and the Indians, despairing, were flinging themselves over the edge of the mesa to doom. The cacique Zutucapan perished in combat, and with his death the spirit of rebellion went out of Ácoma. The shouts of warfare died away; as night fell the only sounds to be heard were the groans of the wounded, the sobbing of the women, the crackle of flames eating through the centuries-old beams of the pueblo. A thousand Indians were dead; the remaining five-hundred people of Ácoma were taken prisoner; the pueblo was wholly destroyed. Vicente de Zaldívar had lost just two of his seventy men in the sacking of Ácoma.

The defeated Indians were herded across the desert to San Gabriel to stand trial for insurrection. Two of the captives thwarted their conquerors: they took refuge in a kiva in San Juan, and for three days fought off with stones those who tried to drag them out. Refusing to surrender, they asked for daggers so that they could kill themselves. Oñate would not trust them with weapons, but suggested that they be thrown ropes with which to hang themselves, never imagining that they would do such a thing. To the Spaniards' amazement, the two Indians soon emerged from the kiva with the ropes tied around their necks as nooses, and climbed quickly to the top of a tree, where they fastened the ropes to a branch. Crying out bitterly, "Our towns, our things, our lands are yours," they called down the vengeance of the gods on the invaders of their country, and, flinging themselves down, died.

The others were tried and speedily found guilty, and Oñate pronounced a frightful sentence. All the men of Ácoma over the age of twenty-five were to have one foot chopped off and then would have to endure twenty years of "personal service" —the dainty Spanish phrase that meant slavery. Two Hopi Indians who had happened to be in Ácoma at the time of the uprising were sentenced to lose their right hands, and then were to be sent back to their homes as living warnings of what would happen to those who defied the might of Spain. Ácoman males between the ages of twelve and twenty-five were spared bodily mutilation, but not the twenty-year term of personal service, and all women of the pueblo over the age of twelve were also condemned to twenty years of slavery.

Under the leadership of old Chumpo, who had opposed the rebellion from the beginning, the people of Ácoma were allowed to build a new pueblo on the plain below their mesa. A few, still hostile, stole back to the mesa-top and took up residence amid the ashes of the old Ácoma, vowing continued defiance of the Spaniards.

The little Spanish colony had survived its first dangerous crisis. Oñate had established Spanish rule in New Mexico through sheer force of personality, in what amounted to a gigantic bluff; four hundred Spaniards could never have withstood a concerted attack by the Indians of all the pueblos, but, by refusing to admit that possibility, Oñate had awed the natives into submission. Ácoma, when it massacred Juan de Zaldívar and his men, had called Oñate's bluff. But the valor and cunning tactics of Vicente de Zaldívar had strengthened the position of the Spaniards; luck had allowed a handful of troops to shatter an entire pueblo, and, though the colonists were as vulnerable as before to a mass attack, the probability that such an attack would ever come had been greatly reduced. The Spaniards, with their guns and their swords and their horses, seemed almost godlike, and few Indians now dared to think of opposing them.

On March 2, 1599, Oñate sent an optimistic report on the colony's prospects to the viceroy in Mexico City. He described New Mexico as

> a land abounding in flesh of buffalo [bison], goats with hideous horns, and turkeys; and in Mohoce [the Spanish name for the Hopi district] there is game of all kinds. There are many wild and ferocious beasts, lions, bears, wolves, tigers, ferrets, porcupines, and other animals, whose hides they tan and use. Towards the west there are bees and very white honey, of which I am sending a sample. Besides, there are vegetables, a great abundance of the best and greatest salines in the world, and very great many kinds of very rich ores. . . . There are very fine grape vines, rivers, forests of many oaks, and some cork trees, fruits, melons, grapes, watermelons, Castilian plums, pine-nuts, acorns, ground-nuts, and *coralejo,* which is a delicious fruit, and other wild fruits. There are many and very good fish in this Rio del Norte.

Oñate noted that the people "are in general very comely," and told the viceroy that "their religion consists in worshipping idols, of which they have many; and in their temples, after their own manner, they worship them with fire, painted reeds, feathers, and universal offering of almost everything they get, such as small animals, birds, vegetables, etc. In their government they are free, for although they have some petty captains, they obey them badly and in very few things. . . ."

Certainly Oñate was overenthusiastic in some of his descriptions—there were no lions or tigers in New Mexico, nor any cork trees, and the "very great many kinds of very rich ores" were not destined to produce much wealth for Spain. But he was correct in saying that New Mexico held great promise. Already the colony had taken root and was beginning to expand. Cattle, sheep, horses, and goats grazed along the Rio Grande. Wheat, oats, barley, onions, apples, and peas were sprouting on the settlers' farms. Children were born. The alien land was losing its mystery. The Indians, sobered by the fate of Ácoma, made no trouble for the strangers in their midst. A network of relationship began to form; some of the Indians went to work for the white men, breaking the soil, helping to build houses. There was trade between the two populations: the Indians exchanged their surplus food for Spanish goods, including wool from the Spaniards' sheep, which they wove into garments that they sold to the colonists.

But the dream of quick and easy treasure still tempted Oñate; gold and pearls seemed more attractive than the profits of a farming society. In the summer of 1600 he sent Vicente de Zaldívar with twenty-five men on another expedition in search of the Pacific. Before starting westward, Zaldívar went to the district in the southeast where the salt deposits were, to gather supplies for his journey. At a village of the Jumano Indians, a non-Pueblo tribe, Zaldívar asked for corn and beans, and was given a shower of stones. He sent word of this to the capital, and Oñate went in person with 50 soldiers to punish the defiant natives. After a battle in which six Indians died, he hanged two Jumano chiefs and burned the village. Zaldívar, continuing into the west, got deep into Arizona before being halted by impassable mountains and savage, hostile Indian tribes. Undaunted Oñate began to plan still another western expedition, which he would lead himself in the spring of 1601.

At Christmas, 1600, a caravan from Mexico reached San

Gabriel. It brought many new colonists, six additional friars, and ample supplies of ammunition, arms, blankets, and shoes. The Spanish population of New Mexico now was more than five hundred. Oñate's reports to the viceroy in Mexico City show continued satisfaction with the growth of the colony: the harvest was good, a flour mill was now in operation, the Indians were "peaceful, undisturbed, and obedient," and the friars' program of baptism was going forward rapidly in the pueblos.

Not everyone shared the governor's rosy view of life in Spanish New Mexico, though. In March, 1601, the same messenger who bore Oñate's latest cheerful report to the viceroy carried a secret letter from one of Oñate's officers, Captain Luís Gasco de Velasco. When the colonists were first setting out in 1598, the viceroy had asked Gasco to send him word privately of "all matters that might be in the interest of the service of His Majesty," and Gasco now fulfilled this charge by pouring forth a torrent of complaints.

"We have been here three years," he began, "hoping to discover something of value and importance, which has not been found up to now." The colonial capital was squalid and dilapidated. The weather was either ferociously hot or numbingly cold, with little in between. Oñate had neglected the development of agriculture and livestock-raising in favor of making long expeditions in quest of treasure, but he had found no treasure. The treatment of the Indians, Gasco said, was deplorable: Spaniards entered the pueblos as they pleased, took anything that attracted them, and forced the natives to work as if they were slaves. The colonists had exacted so much food from them that many villages were close to starvation. On the slightest provocation, according to Gasco, Oñate would inflict cruel punishments on the Indians—the prime example being the burning of Ácoma and the subsequent mutilation of its adult men. The trouble at Ácoma, Gasco claimed, had been started by Spanish soldiers in the first place. Nor was it any cause for pride that a handful of Spaniards had been able to defeat a whole province of Indians, for these Pueblo folk were "the most meek, humble, and timid people ever seen."

Gasco also declared that Oñate had turned haughty and irrational, and seemed to rule "according to his own whim and that of his nephew," Vicente de Zaldívar. He had put to death several soldiers who he thought were conspiring against him, and had begun to conduct himself as though he were a king and not merely a governor. On several occasions he had shown disrespect for royal authority, and—a truly serious accusation—Gasco said that he had been "amazed and stunned" to hear Vicente de Zaldívar address Oñate as "Your Majesty."

Very likely Gasco's secret report was an exaggerated account of Oñate's failings; just as likely, things were not going as well in New Mexico as Oñate believed. Certainly many of the colonists felt that Oñate was devoting too much time to his expeditions and not enough to the immediate needs of the colony. Some were embittered because Oñate had promised to lead them into a land of gold and silver, and instead seemed to have brought them to a place where the only hope of survival lay in scratching a living from corn and beans. And one faction, made up largely of priests, felt that he had been altogether too harsh on the Indians, particularly in the case of the people of Ácoma. In the spring of 1601, as Oñate prepared for his next attempt to reach the Pacific, San Gabriel was a tense, divided town. But Oñate does not seem to have been aware of the words being spoken against him in his own capital.

At the last minute he changed his plans: he would go

northeast instead of west, and look for the gold of Quivira instead of the pearls of the Pacific. Ever since Coronado's futile trek of 1541, Quivira had proved to be a mere phantom for all who had sought it, but Oñate had fallen victim to a familiar Spanish disease, the feverish lust for precious metal, which left him beyond the reach of logic. His departure was delayed, though, by another unhappy incident: while gathering salt in the southeast, a group of Spanish soldiers was attacked by Indians of the Piro-speaking pueblo of Quarai, and two Spaniards were killed. Oñate reacted in a familiar way, sending Vicente de Zaldívar with a large force to avenge the slayings. For five days and nights Quarai held the Spaniards off despite immense losses; forty of Zaldívar's men were wounded, and Zaldívar himself suffered a broken arm. In the end the pueblo was forced to surrender when the Spaniards cut its water supply. The town was burned; nine hundred Indians had perished and two hundred were captured.

In June, 1601, when the Quarai affair was finished, Oñate set out for Quivira with two friars and nearly eighty soldiers. The project was a severe drain on the colony's slender resources, for the governor took with him seven hundred horses and mules, a great deal of food, and a staff of Indians to carry the baggage. Through month after month Oñate wandered through the boundless plains, deep into what now is Kansas. The Indians were generally unfriendly and he was forced to fight several major battles. As for the fabled gold, the Indians always said he would find it in the next town north, or the one after that, but it was never there.

During Oñate's absence San Gabriel was in ferment. A mass meeting of the colonists in July led to a general denunciation of Oñate. He had, said one settler after another, squandered the colony's strength on foolish explorations, needlessly angered the Indians by excessive harshness, and become increasingly high-handed in his method of governing; worst of all, he had failed to make his people rich. A phrase originally uttered seventy years before by Oñate's wife's grandfather, the conqueror Cortés, was frequently quoted: "I came to get gold, not to till the soil like a peasant." All but a handful of the colonists expressed a wish to give up and go back to Mexico. In September, most of them did just that, packing their meager belongings and abandoning San Gabriel. After a two-month journey southward, the deserters reached the Mexican town of Santa Barbara and told the story of the breakup of the colony to the viceroy's representatives there.

Late in November, 1601, Oñate returned to San Gabriel, coming home weary and empty-handed from Quivira. He was astounded to find only a ghost town remaining. A few dozen loyal settlers had remained; the others, he learned, had fled to Mexico. Infuriated, he ordered Vicente de Zaldívar to go after the renegades and force them to come back. But when Zaldívar reached Mexico, the authorities informed him that the former colonists were under no legal obligation to resume their lives in New Mexico.

Oñate's world was crumbling. Quivira was a myth; the mines of Arizona went unexploited for lack of men to work in them; even the hope of creating an agricultural empire on the Rio Grande now seemed dead. The only remaining possibility was to reach the Pacific, harvest the pearls that the Indians claimed could be found there, and develop ports from which merchant vessels belonging to New Mexico could take part in the profitable trade with the Spanish outposts in the Philippine Islands and China. But for that he needed manpower. In 1602 Oñate sent the indefatigable Vicente de Zaldívar to Spain to beg aid from the king.

At Madrid Zaldívar spoke of the potential importance of

New Mexico as a Spanish base and defended his uncle's administration against the charges of the deserters. He asked the king for four hundred soldiers, a corps of skilled shipbuilders to construct the vessels for Pacific trade, a loan of money, and new settlers. For two years these requests shuttled through the royal bureaucracy, while, unknown to Zaldívar, an investigation into the conduct of Oñate proceeded secretly. At one point Oñate's enemies succeeded in having the colony abolished by royal decree; later it was reinstated, but the government declined to invest men or money in it. Zaldívar came home with nothing to show for his journey. The colony was still alive, but only barely.

In a kind of desperation Oñate decided to go to the Pacific even with his mere skeleton crew. He left in October, 1604, with thirty men, marching westward into Arizona to find the Colorado River, then following it to its mouth on the Gulf of California. This was not exactly the Pacific, for California itself still lay to the west; but at that time it was believed that California was an island, and Oñate thought he had come to the sea. After finding a fine harbor in January, 1605, he turned back toward New Mexico and reached San Gabriel three months later.

The Spanish government, meanwhile, was again considering making an end to the shaky colony. The Mexican viceroy had recommended to the king in 1605 that New Mexico be abandoned, arguing that there was little hope of finding important quantities of gold and silver there, and that the land was not really worth farming. The king, however, replied that even though no profit could come from New Mexico, the colony should be allowed to continue, if only for the sake of bringing the benefits of Christianity to the Indians. But all costly expeditions to distant parts of the province in search of treasure were to cease at once, and

Oñate was to be removed from office. "You shall, with tact and discretion," the king instructed his viceroy, "cause the said Don Juan de Oñate to be recalled [to Mexico] for some sufficient reason, as seems best to you, so that he may come without disturbance. . . ." Once Oñate had reached Mexico, some pretext was to be found for keeping him there permanently, while another man replaced him in the colony.

Realizing what was happening, Oñate resisted the summons to come to Mexico, but after several years of legal maneuvering he found himself with no choice but to yield. In 1609 he left San Gabriel for the last time, riding south in disgrace. Fourteen years had passed since he first had asked for the right to colonize New Mexico. The expenses of the project had devoured his once considerable fortune, and the dispute over his capacity to govern the colony had clouded his high reputation. There was one final bitter thrust as he turned his back on New Mexico. As Oñate's party traveled through the desert below the southernmost pueblo, a band of Indians attacked, and one Spanish soldier was killed in the skirmish: Oñate's only son. The former governor buried him and journeyed onward toward Mexico; and there the reward for his service to the king was trial, in 1614, for "crimes and excesses." Indicted for innumerable violations of law, he was acquitted on most charges, but found guilty on some, including an accusation of inhumane severity against the Indians of Ácoma. The sentence was a fine of six thousand golden ducats and perpetual exile from New Mexico. Oñate appealed the decision to the Council of the Indies, the highest governmental body in Spanish America, and, after seven years, the Council recommended that he be pardoned. The king took no action on his case, however, and in 1624 Oñate sailed to Spain to plead for clemency at court. He was now more than seventy-five years old. At Madrid he finally found pity: a full pardon, and even a new government office, inspector of mines for the Spanish home government. His few remaining years are unrecorded by history.

The colony he had founded still endured. From its low point in 1601, after the desertion of most of the original settlers from San Gabriel, it had gradually regained strength; in his final year of power, 1608, Oñate had managed to bring in a number of new colonists, so that New Mexico's Spanish population was nearly back to what it had been at the beginning.

Don Pedro de Peralta, Oñate's successor as governor, abandoned the unhappy first capital of San Gabriel, and founded the new city of Sante Fe in 1610. Its full name was *Villa Real de la Sante Fe de San Francisco de Asis,* "Royal City of the Holy Faith of St. Francis of Assisi." The site Peralta chose was not on the Rio Grande, but rather on one of its tributaries, a river that was named the Santa Fe. Set among the foothills of the Sangre de Cristo Mountains, the new capital literally rose above the humble villages of the Indians strung along the Rio Grande, not far to the west. Santa Fe held a central location in the Pueblo world, with the Tewa-speaking and Keres-speaking towns clustered about it. To the north lay such important pueblos as San Juan, San Ildefonso, and Taos; to the south were Santo Domingo— where the Franciscan fathers had established New Mexico's religious headquarters—and the Tiguex group. The buildings of Santa Fe were adobe ones, tawny and attractive, arranged around a spacious, handsome plaza. The most impressive of them was the palace of Governor Peralta, a long, noble structure on the plaza, which was destined to serve as the residence of New Mexico's governors for three hundred years before becoming a museum early in the twentieth century; today it is regarded as the finest monument of New Mexico's colonial period.

Under the new administration, fantasies of gold and pearls were laid aside. The Spaniards of New Mexico concentrated on two projects: squeezing a living from the soil, and converting the Indians to Christianity. These goals often came into conflict, for the economy of the colony could not be put on a functioning basis without exploiting the natives, while the friars saw it as their duty to protect their newly baptized Indian parishioners against such exploitation. Two parallel and rival governments sprang up in New Mexico—the civil government in Santa Fe, and the church government in Santo Domingo—and through much of the seventeenth century the peace of the colony was torn by the struggle between the two powers, between those who were the deputies of the King of Spain and those who were the deputies of God.

The growth of the church in New Mexico was steady and strong. A few dozen friars spread out through the pueblos, going in ones and twos to every village of the province, bringing word of Christ to the Indians. They were dedicated, courageous men, who courted martyrdom as a routine part of their daily work, and the natives responded to the bravery and sturdiness of these patient, fearless missionaries. In each pueblo the friar won the attention of the Indians by retelling the most dramatic tales of the Bible: the Christmas story, the crucifixion, the wandering of the Israelites in the desert, the creation of Adam and Eve. Storytelling was an intimate part of the Pueblo religious life, and this treasure trove of strange new legends excited the imaginations of the Indians. Then the priests explained the more complex aspects of Christianity: that each human being has an immortal soul, that Christ was sent to the world by His father to redeem man from sin, that the religion of Jesus was a creed of love and compassion. Because they were Franciscans, who particularly revered the gentle St. Francis, the themes of love and compassion were strong in their teachings, and they charmed the Indians with their stories of the saint's simplicity, his self-denial, his tenderness toward all living things.

Over the sharp and furious opposition of the conservative men of the pueblos, the heads of the secret societies, the guardians of the native religion, the Indians began to accept baptism and learn the tenets of the Christian faith. The friars taught them more than just theology, though: they instructed the Indians in the Spanish ways of agriculture and raising livestock, in carpentry, in music, in painting, in sculpture.

The Indians employed their new skills to build churches and mission houses for their priests. By 1617 there were eleven churches in New Mexico, and the friars were claiming fourteen thousand converts. In the next ten years more than thirty new churches arose; some pueblos, like Taos in the far north, held out against Christianity for a long time, but in time Taos got its church. And in 1629 even Ácoma, where bitterness against the Spaniards ran understandably deep, allowed the construction of a church on the mesa-top after Fray Juan Ramirez miraculously cured a sick Indian child.

It was no small church that went up at Ácoma, nor was it any easy thing for the Indians to haul such immense logs to their mesa's lofty summit; the house they built for the god of the Spaniards was a magnificent edifice. So was it done everywhere in the colony. The churches were twenty to forty feet wide, sixty to one hundred feet long, with adobe walls many feet thick and roofs made of huge beams. Under the guidance of the friar the Indian carpenters made doors and doorframes, window moldings, altars, crosses. On the white-washed walls of the church's interior the people painted bright murals: birds, flowers, symbols of the sun, the rain, the lightning, abstract forms, the whole lively repertoire of expressive native artists. Adjoining the church were the mission buildings, the priest's house, a cloister, classrooms, servants' quarters. In the mission's garden the friar planted grapevines that had been shipped from Spain to Mexico, from Mexico to New Mexico, and from the grapes he made the wines used in the holy sacraments. In the garden, too, were orchards of fruit unfamiliar to the Pueblo folk: pears, peaches, figs, dates, pomegranates, olives, cherries, quinces, lemons, oranges, nectarines.

The church became the new center of the pueblo. The friar, the source of all the wondrous alien knowledge, was constantly surrounded by his flock, asking questions, showing off what they had learned. When the churchbells rang, the people gathered for the service; they knelt before the altar, looked up in awe at the image of Christ on the cross, at the paintings showing the saints and angels, and murmured in uncertain Latin their responses to the priest's words. By 1630 the head of the Franciscan mission to New Mexico was able to report to the king that fifty friars were at work in ninety native villages, both of Pueblo and non-Pueblo Indians, and that each village had its own church. Some sixty thousand Indians had been baptized by this time, even some of the wild and nomadic Navaho and Apache who roamed the outskirts of the pueblo region.

The acceptance of Christianity, though, did not mean that the Pueblo Indians were giving up their old religion. The kiva and the church flourished side by side. A strange doubleness of life developed: the pueblos acquired Spanish names, Santa Clara and San Ildefonso and Santo Domingo and San Juan, and the people used those names, but at the same time they went on calling their villages Xapogeh and Poxwogeh and Kiua and Caypa. The friars baptized the Indians with good Spanish names like Juan Padilla and Gregorio Herrera, but those were "Sunday" names, and Juan and Gregorio continued to go by their native names. Crosses and portraits of Jesus appeared in their homes, but the old pagan statuettes and symbols remained. As the anthropologist Matilda Stevenson wrote in 1894 after many years of studying the Indians of the Rio Grande pueblos, they

> are in fact as non-Catholic as before the Spanish conquest. ... [They] have preserved their religion ... holding their ceremonials in secret, practicing their occult powers to the present time, under the very eye of the church. ... The Catholic priest marries the betrothed, but they have been previously united according to their ancestral rites. The Romish priest holds mass that the dead may enter heaven, but prayers have already been offered that the soul may be received by Sus-sis-tin-na-ko (their creator) into the lower world. ... Though professedly Catholic, they wait only the departure of the priest to return to their secret ceremonials.

The rituals of the Pueblos have lost much of their meaning for the younger Indians of our own day, but they still are observed by these supposedly Christian people, and the rites performed today are probably not very different from those of the seventeenth century, or those of the time before the friars came. Erna Fergusson, a New Mexico woman who has entered closely into Pueblo life and ceremonies, wrote in her book *Dancing Gods* of 1931, "Their religion is of earth and the things of earth. I thought of all these brown people whom I had seen dancing their prayers, pounding them with their feet into the earth, which is their mother. Her ways are close to them, even when they are hurt. They understand the earth, they dance their prayers into the earth, and they pray for real things, for sun, and rain and corn. For growth—for life."

All the year long there are rituals that must be performed —at planting time, during the time when the crops are growing, at harvest time, and after the harvest, when thanks are due. Rain gives life to the crops, and rain is the gift of the gods. If the ceremonies are neglected, the gods will cease to watch over the pueblo, the rain will not fall, the corn will shrivel in the fields.

Pueblo religion is a community affair. A man does not pray alone. If he fears a dry summer, he takes part in the rain dances. If his child is ill, he sends for the men of the medicine society, who cure him—or try to—through ritual. The rites govern everything in village life: birth, marriage, sickness, death, the yield of the fields, success in war, safety in travel. The ceremonies are lengthy—many of them take several weeks to perform completely—and usually consist of dramatizations of mythological events dealing with the creation and early migrations of the tribe. The kiva is the place where much of the ritual is acted out. Often the men remain in the kiva for days on end, emerging into the plaza of the pueblo only at the climax of the ceremony.

No village has full-time priests of the native religion. The rituals are performed by every adult. Certain men lead, because they are older and wiser in the sacred ways and have been initiated into the secret societies that have responsibility for the various ceremonies. But when the rites are over, these men who have served as priests return to the everyday task of earning a living.

The Pueblo child becomes aware of his village's religious life early in childhood. He sees his father going off to spend days or even weeks in the kiva. He hears the sound of chanting and drumming. Then—most exciting and frightening of all—he sees the masked gods enter the pueblo and begin to dance.

The masked gods are known in every pueblo by the Hopi term, *kachinas*. They are awesome as they arrive, weirdly costumed, ornamented with horns or parrot feathers or evergreen boughs, their bodies painted and glistening. Some kachinas move with stately, somber tread, others caper and run and hop. The procession moves about the plaza while the villagers watch in silence. Kachinas armed with yucca-leaf whips drive the crowds back, keeping them from getting too close to the dancers.

The fantastic, flamboyant figures are nightmare creatures, grotesque, terrifying, unreal. To the Pueblos they are supernatural beings who live far away and visit the pueblos to bring rain. Though the kachina legend differs in detail from village to village, all agree that long ago the kachina spirits lived with men, teaching hunting and farming and the arts and crafts; and when the people needed rain, the kachinas danced in the fields to bring it. But in time there was a quarrel between kachinas and men, and the kachinas went to dwell in their distant home. Now they come back only at festival time, to bring the rain.

The Pueblo child watches these strange beings parading in the plaza, and the sight instills an awareness that the spirit world is never very far away. As he grows up he is given dolls that represent the various kachinas. There are more than three hundred of them, each with a distinctive headdress and appearance. These are not toys; they are part of a child's religious education, a kind of catechism.

Later, when a boy is twelve or thirteen, he learns the secret of the kachinas. He is taken to a kiva by his parents or grandparents. Kachinas are present; one of the older men of the pueblo explains their importance, and then the terrified boy is lightly whipped by the bizarre apparitions. But then comes the great revelation. The masks are lifted from the kachinas' heads, and the boy sees that the masked gods are really just members of the pueblo, men he has known all his life. It is a little like discovering that there is no Santa Claus. The leader of the group now declares that the kachinas themselves no longer come to the pueblos: they have given the people permission to wear masks and impersonate them. When men of the village don the kachina masks and perform the proper dances, the kachina spirits enter them and rain comes.

The boy is given his own kachina mask. Now he is regarded as an adult, and begins to take part in the ceremonies of the pueblo. Girls are almost never initiated into the kachina cult, though they are allowed to know the secret. After he has been taught the mysteries of the kachinas, a Pueblo boy may join one of the secret societies of his village, although this is not required. Perhaps he will become a member of the "clown" societies, whose members frolic and cavort during the dances, deliberately breaking the solemnity. Perhaps he will join a society that specializes in handling venomous snakes, or one whose members eat fire, thrusting flaming sticks in their mouths, or one that has the duty of healing the sick. All are part of the religious life of the community.

It was this religion of kachinas and secret societies that the Franciscan missionaries hoped to replace with the worship of the Christian God. At first, seeing the eagerness with which the Indians were accepting their teachings, it seemed as if the friars were successful. Only gradually did the priests realize that the kiva still thrived. Some, then, counseled patience: given time, Jesus would prevail over the masked gods. Others, in their frustration, urged that the native religion be stamped out by force. The debate became a passionate one—and helped to contribute, in time, to the tragedy of seventeenth-century New Mexico.

5

The Troubled Colony

BY 1624 the Spanish population of New Mexico had reached two thousand. The colony seemed permanently established, but its development was sluggish, and it appeared doomed always to be no more than a scrawny and pitiful appendage to Spain's flourishing Mexican realm. About a thousand settlers, at most, lived in and around Santa Fe, and the rest were scattered up and down the Rio Grande in tiny towns or occasional isolated estates.

To encourage colonization, Governor Oñate had introduced a system of land grants known as *encomiendas,* which was widely employed in Mexico and other provinces of Spain's American empire. Encomiendas were tracts of land which the governor awarded to men who had taken part in the conquest and expansion of the colony; the largest and best encomiendas, naturally, went to the key members of the colonial administration. In a sense, all the land used for encomiendas had been seized from the Indians, but generally the land that was parceled out was selected from that not in use by the natives. However, some of the encomiendas were quite close to the pueblos, and took in land that the Indians might soon have been farming for themselves.

With the encomienda went the right of *repartimiento,* which was the privilege of employing Indians to farm the land grants. Under Spanish law, Indian labor was supposed to be voluntary, and those who volunteered were supposed to be paid for their work. But in practice a kind of feudalism emerged; the Indians were virtually serfs, bound to the land and receiving no payment except, perhaps, a small share of the farm produce. The *encomenderos,* or proprietors of the encomiendas, were forbidden by law to live on the lands they held, but this law also was generally ignored, so that the encomenderos became landed aristocrats, many of them living on *haciendas,* large estates, with platoons of native servants to farm their lands and wait upon their needs. The Indians were compelled to pay tribute in corn and cloth by way of showing their obligation to their master, the King of Spain, and also were called upon to offer periods of personal service, which grew longer and longer each year, until they were little more than slaves. Indians now tended the white man's crops, looked after his cattle and goats, and worked as unpaid laborers in his factories, turning out cotton shirts, woolen blankets, and other articles of cloth, wool, and hides which the colonists marketed for a good price in Mexico. A share of the profits went to Spain, as the king's fifth; the rest enriched the settlers.

The governor of the colony was usually the most dedicated exploiter. He interpreted his official status as a license to amass as much wealth as possible; thus he pushed the Indians as far as he dared, so that after the requirements of tribute to the king had been met, his own share would be enormous. Since his powers were virtually absolute, he was able to demand a share of each encomendero's profits, as well as awarding himself the exclusive right to import (and sell at high prices) many of the goods needed by the settlers. Governor after governor ran New Mexico as a private business, not as a province of an imperial nation.

Since the friars, too, had need of Indian labor, there were frequent quarrels between the priests at Santo Domingo and the governors at Santa Fe. The missionaries not only had humanitarian objections to the abuse of the natives, but also felt that the colonists and civil authorities were draining the energies of the Indians so severely that they would not be able to serve the requirements of the church in proper fashion. If the governor compelled the Indians to work to the point of exhaustion and starvation on the lands of the encomenderos, who would tend the orchards of the missions? Who would build new churches and maintain the old ones? Who would provide the priests and their growing staffs with food?

Both the moral questions and these more selfish ones led to a bitter struggle between "the two Majesties"—the crown and the church—over the handling of the Indians. The Spaniards had come to New Mexico both to get rich and to serve God, and where these aims were opposed, trouble resulted.

It was difficult for the Spanish civil authorities or the ordinary Spanish settler to see the Indians as anything much more than beasts of burden, placed upon the earth to carry out the bidding of Europeans; clearly they were some kind of inferior species, for they had no apparent ambitions or desires, showed no interest in wealth or fine ornaments, did not care to expand their territory at the expense of their neighbors—in fact, seemed content to eat and sleep. Why not make use of these placid, docile creatures to help build the empire for the greater glory of Spain and the higher profits of her citizens?

But the churchmen, though they too demanded service from the Indians, regarded them primarily as human beings with immortal souls, capable at least potentially of being the equal of any man of Toledo or Madrid. As the sixteenth-century priest Bartolomé de las Casas, a most passionate defender of the rights of the Indians in the period of the conquest of the New World, put it: "They neither possess nor desire to possess worldly wealth. Surely these people would be the most blessed in the world if only they worshipped the true God." And a decree of Pope Paul III in 1537 had branded the notion that "Indians should be treated as dumb brutes created for our service" as the teaching of the Devil. The Pope had insisted "that the Indians are truly men and that they are not only capable of understanding the Catholic faith but, according to our information, they desire exceedingly to receive it. . . ." Whether or not the Indians chose to remain outside the Christian religion, though, the Pope declared, they "are by no means to be deprived of their liberty or the possession of their property . . . nor should they be in any way enslaved."

The civil authorities of Spanish America gave lip-service to these doctrines, but in practice they drew the Indians gradually but steadily into a state of slavery as the manpower needs of the colonies required. This gradual process, when it began to take place in New Mexico, led to increased friction between the government and the church, and by 1613 "the two Majesties" were engaged in something very much like civil war.

In that year Governor Peralta dispatched a platoon of soldiers to the pueblo of Taos to collect the regular tribute of farm produce, which was overdue. When the troops arrived, they were confronted by Fray Isidro Ordóñez, the father-president, or head, of the church in New Mexico. Fray

Isidro told the Indians of Taos to ignore the request for tribute, and ordered the soldiers to go back empty-handed to Santa Fe. He also expressed his displeasure over Peralta's use of forced Indian labor in the construction of the governor's palace in the new capital. Governor Peralta, enraged, denounced Fray Isidro in such violent terms that the father-president called down on him the church's most severe penalty: excommunication. Calling Peralta "a heretic, a Lutheran, and a Jew"—thus characterizing him in rhetorical terms as an outcast from Catholicism—Fray Isidro banned him from receiving any of the sacraments of the Christian faith. At a stormy meeting between the two men a few weeks later, Peralta drew his pistol and fired at the father-president, missing him by a narrow margin and hitting another friar and a civilian. Fray Isidro demanded that the town council of Santa Fe arrest and punish the governor for this assault, but no action was taken.

Fray Isidro then sent word of Peralta's misconduct to Mexico City, while declaring that anyone who attempted to carry a message to Mexico telling Peralta's side of the story would be excommunicated. Peralta, thereupon, set out for Mexico himself to win the viceroy's aid against the troublesome priest, only to be seized by the father-president's agents near the pueblo of Isleta, in the south, and thrown into chains at a convent. Fray Isidro, in effect, had seized control of New Mexico. No one dared to oppose him. Peralta escaped from the convent and returned to Santa Fe, but was swiftly arrested and imprisoned again. Chaos threatened to engulf the colony. At the height of the confusion Fray Isidro granted permission for all settlers and soldiers who wished to return to Mexico to go; as a result, the population of Santa Fe dropped to forty-seven, outside of priests.

By this time word of the state of things in New Mexico had

come to the viceroy in Mexico City. In May, 1614, a new governor, Admiral Bernardo de Ceballos, arrived in Santa Fe to replace Peralta; and, after one of the New Mexican friars went to Mexico to protest that Fray Isidro had overstepped his authority, the viceroy had him replaced as well. A kind of order came to New Mexico again.

But the basic issue over which the officials at Santa Fe and the friars at Santo Domingo had quarreled remained unresolved. In the eyes of the colonial government, the priests were building up a rival power within the territory, draining the strength of the Indians in the construction and maintenance of churches, and interfering with the proper purpose of the colony, which was to reap profits. In the eyes of the priests, the colonial government was heartlessly misusing the services of the Indians, who were Christians under the protection of the Pope.

Each side continually tried to undermine the authority of the other. Since the Indians were plainly more sympathetic to the friars who defended them than to the settlers who exploited them, the governors did their best to drive a wedge between the missionaries and the natives. One particularly sinister tactic was introduced in 1619 by Admiral de Ceballos' successor, Governor Eulate. He encouraged the Indians to revive their kachinas, their pagan dances, their whole system of religious festivals. The priests, of course, were alarmed by this resurgence of the old native religion, and some of them took extreme measures to prevent the Indians from slipping away from Christianity. In a few pueblos, kivas were burned, and masks and sacred images were thrown on the fires. The old religious practices were sternly forbidden. This had the effect of turning the Indians against the suddenly intolerant priests, which was exactly what Governor Eulate hoped to accomplish. The more strictly the friars tried to suppress the old creed, the greater the resentment of the Indians toward them, and the easier it became for Santa Fe to impose its own power on the villagers.

Through the 1620's and 1630's the friars complained constantly to the viceroy, to the king, and to their own superiors in the church about the abuses of the colonial government. One governor, they reported, forced the Indians to undergo terrible marches through the desert, carrying on their backs immense loads of salt from the salines east of the mountains, and this, they told the viceroy, "has occasioned among the natives serious illnesses and convulsions, some of them being permanently incapacitated . . . both on account of the haste and misfortunes attending their departure, and because of the long distance which they carried the salt." Indians were taken from their homes to serve on distant encomiendas; they were compelled to give, aside from this personal service, immense tributes in corn and cotton cloth; some were even sold into slavery in Mexico.

Another memorandum of complaint dealt with the visit of a certain government official to an eastern pueblo where the Indians of the choir were about to assemble for the celebration of the high mass. At his order the whole choir was whipped, and "the poor things have not since then dared to take part in any sung mass, wherefore the divine service has been impeded." The same official, while at the pueblo of Quarai, heard the Indians ask permission to help reap the harvest at the mission's wheatfield. According to the friars' complaint, this official angrily commanded the Indians "not to reap the wheat nor serve the father, for if they did he would give them one hundred lashes; for such was the command of his governor. . . ."

Luring the Indians away from Christianity was not always done so bluntly. At one pueblo in the west some captains from Santa Fe went among the Indians, and one of them proclaimed "that the people should come together, for he had some things to tell them which were very sweet, very pleasant, and very much in accord with their desires." The friars did not know what the officer said to the Indians, "but from that time they did not ring the Ave Maria, or the evening bells, nor did they attend the teaching of the doctrine or the choir, but acted as if they had never been converted. . . ."

What disturbed the priests most of all was the way the governors openly urged the Indians to revive their old religious dances. The frenzied outcries of the dancers and the apparent ecstasy they experienced made these dances seem truly devilish and sinister: "The Indians appear beside themselves, though no drinking has taken place whereby they may have become intoxicated." Appalled by the renewed practice of these barbaric-seeming pagan rites, the shocked priests desperately tried to halt them. We are told that Fray Salvador de Guerra, the pastor of the pueblo of Isleta, "went throughout the pueblo with a cross upon his shoulders, a crown of thorns, and a rope about his neck, beating his bare body, in order that they might stop the dance." After a while the Indians "came after him weeping, and saying they were not to blame, because the governor had commanded them to do as they were doing."

The governors, when queried by Mexico City about these serious charges, replied with charges of their own. The friars, they said, were hypocrites who exploited and mistreated the Indians themselves—whipping those who failed to attend mass regularly, severely punishing those who innocently broke some minor church rule, and otherwise arbitrarily interfering with the rhythms of village life. Many of the priests were accused of being drunkards or worse. And the priests were greedy, the governors claimed—making the Indians work like beasts to support them.

Between 1637 and 1641, when Don Luis de Rosas was governor, the split between church and crown grew wider than it had been at any time since the Peralta crisis of 1613. In his attempt to weaken the power of the friars, Rosas succeeded in keeping New Mexico's missions understaffed, so that many churches went without any priest at all for months or even years. He stirred such enmity against the friars among the Indians that the people of the pueblo of Jemez murdered their missionary. At Taos, the Indians not only killed the priest but wrecked the church. Although the records of the period are sketchy and unclear, it seems as though the priests were instrumental in organizing a conspiracy against Governor Rosas, which brought about his assassination in 1641.

Don Bernardo López de Mendizábal, New Mexico's governor in the 1650's, followed the example of some of his predecessors in trying to hamper the friars by encouraging the performance of the native ceremonials. He declared publicly that he looked upon the kachina dances as mere "Indian foolishness," and could see no harm in them. When he visited the pueblos, he allowed the Indians to do their dances for him as a means of honoring his presence. He told the people of several pueblos that he regarded it as quite proper for them to go on observing their ancient rituals even though they now were Christians, and in one whimsical moment he said that if it were not for the necessity of upholding his dignity as governor, he would go out and dance with the Indians himself.

López clearly was going too far. A royal governor could not cheerfully speak out in favor of idolatry and paganism. New Mexico's father-president of the time protested to

Mexico City and to that grim investigative arm of the church, the Holy Office of the Inquisition. Although the governmental authorities in Mexico City seemed to feel that permitting the dances would not endanger the Indians' souls, the Inquisition felt otherwise, and, entangled in religious controversy, Governor López was forced to resign his office in 1660.

His successor was Don Diego de Peñalosa Briceña, a flamboyant, eccentric character who made it clear at once that he intended to rule over New Mexico in regal style. As he set out for Mexico, Peñalosa sent word ahead that when he reached Senecú, the first inhabited pueblo north of the Rio Grande crossing at El Paso del Norte, he expected all settlers for fifty leagues around to be there to meet him and accompany him in grand procession to Santa Fe. About two hundred colonists obeyed. The friars at Senecú rang their churchbells to greet him as he approached, and the pueblo's main priest showed his respect for the new governor by humbly waiting for him at the gate outside the mission; but Peñalosa loudly criticized the priest for not having marched out to meet him when he was still six miles down the road. "What ridiculous pretensions for his reception!" the priest complained in a protest to Mexico City.

After stopping at pueblo after pueblo, forcing each mission to entertain him in a ruinously costly fashion, Peñalosa at last took up residence in the governor's palace at Santa Fe. One of his first orders was that each pueblo must send him an Indian trumpet player once a week to play for him in the palace while he dined. Equally ostentatious decrees followed.

The friars, meanwhile, were taking advantage of the change in governors to undo the damage caused by Governor López' tolerance of pagan rituals. In 1661, the father-president, Fray Alonso de Posada, imposed strict new rules on every pueblo. The kachina dances were absolutely prohibited, and the missionaries were told to seek out and destroy all implements of "idolatry." The kivas were raided, and 1,600 kachina masks were seized and destroyed, along with prayer feathers, kachina dolls, and sacred images of other kinds. The harshness with which this purge was carried out left the Pueblo folk tense and resentful; now that the early gentleness of the missionaries had given way to the imposition of Christianity by force and the stern abolition of the old religion, there were whispers of revolt in the villages. The Pueblos had been willing to take on Christianity in addition to their own beliefs, just as they had been willing to let the Spaniards establish a system of pueblo government alongside their own; but the show of intolerance that had sprung from the quarrel between the missionaries and the governors was leading them to regret ever having allowed the Spaniards to enter their land.

Governor Peñalosa, once he realized what the missionaries were doing, took the customary means of checking the authority of the priests. When one friar went to Taos to rebuild the ruined church, Peñalosa appointed as governor of that pueblo the very Indian who had murdered the previous priest, and decreed that any Taos Indian who helped to reconstruct the church would be put to death. The missionary was forced to withdraw and Taos remained without a church. When friars protested Peñalosa's other anti-missionary decrees, he told them loftily that he had secret instructions to strangle any priest who became too troublesome.

As a result, the colony again became embroiled in virtual warfare between the two Majesties, and a paralysis of government set it. The climax of Peñalosa's turbulent reign came in August, 1663, when the governor sent his soldiers into the church at Santo Domingo to seize an escaped prisoner who had taken sanctuary in it. The right to use a church as sanctuary was one of Christianity's deepest traditions, and Peñalosa's violation of it astonished the entire colony. When the father-president, Fray Alonso, heard of the deed, he ordered the governor to release the prisoner or face excommunication. Peñalosa, who had briefly been a priest himself when a young man, retorted that he "recognized no judge in this country who could excommunicate him, neither ecclesiastic, bishop, nor archbishop." Sending soldiers to the pueblo of Pecos, where Fray Alonso had been staying, he had the father-president taken into custody and brought to Santa Fe to be jailed in the palace.

Then, a little amazed at his own audacity, Peñalosa looked about for some face-saving way of retreating from what he had done. He waited for the friars to request the release of Fray Alonso, intending to grant it immediately; but the friars said nothing, and Peñalosa was forced by his sense of his own dignity to keep the father-president in confinement. Embarrassed and worried, Peñalosa finally asked the pastor to Isleta to call for the freeing of Fray Alonso; the pastor obliged, and in October, 1663, Peñalosa let him go.

The father-president, who was also the resident commissioner of the Holy Office of the Inquisition, promptly filed a blistering complaint with his fellow Inquisitors in Mexico City, and in a short while Peñalosa found it necessary to resign as governor and journey meekly to Mexico to submit to the Inquisition's judgment. After an investigation that lasted several years, he received, in February, 1668, the heaviest sentence the Inquisitors had ever imposed in the New World: to pay a fine of five hundred pesos and all the costs of the investigation, to walk bareheaded and barefoot through the streets of Mexico City carrying a lighted green candle as a symbol of repentance, and to leave the New

World, from which he was perpetually banished, within a month. The Inquisition had to lend him money with which to get back to Europe; once there, he attempted to interest first England and then France in plans for the conquest of Spanish America.

Despite the comic aspects of the Peñalosa episode, it was a serious matter for New Mexico, for it left the relations between the friars and the government more tattered than ever. The Indians, observing the spectacle of open feuding between their supposed spiritual and political masters, developed contempt for the Spaniards, where once they had felt only awe. Increasingly they asked themselves why they tolerated this handful of haughty aliens in their midst. While the missionaries flogged and even hanged the Indians to save their souls, the civil authorities enslaved them, plundered the wealth of their cornfields, forced them to abide by incomprehensible Spanish laws.

There were isolated incidents of revolt. About 1645, the men of one Rio Grande pueblo rebelled after the hanging of forty of their tribesmen who refused to convert to Christianity, but the disturbance was quickly quelled. At another pueblo, Jemez, a Spaniard was killed in an uprising, and in return the governor hanged twenty-nine Indians and imprisoned many more as "witches."

In the west, where the Spaniards never were able to assert the same degree of control, that they held over the Rio Grande villages, violent outbursts were less frequent. The Zuni Indians did not receive their first missionaries until 1629, when four priests arrived; these were tolerated for several years, but in 1633 the Zuni killed two of them, along with their military escort. (Ten years later missions were successfully reestablished at two of the Zuni pueblos.) The Hopi also killed a friar in 1633, after having shown strong resistance to conversion; but the missionaries persevered and introduced their religion. At the pueblo of Oraibi the Hopi were forced to haul logs from a forest forty miles away to built the huge mission. They called it "the slave church" and secretly went on worshipping the kachinas. When a friar caught a Hopi in "an act of idolatry" at Oraibi in 1655, he thrashed the man until blood came, then poured burning turpentine over him. The man died; when the Indians complained, the friar was transferred to a different district. Another priest, unwilling to drink water from the springs around Oraibi, demanded that his water be brought from a source fifty miles distant. However, since both the Hopi and the Zuni were too far away from the main Spanish settlement to suffer much exploitation, they generally remained tranquil during the decades when tensions were mounting along the Rio Grande.

The increasing difficulties among Spaniards and between Spaniard and Indian were not the only problems for New Mexico in the second half of the seventeenth century. Beginning in 1660, the skies began to withhold their favor. Drought gripped the Southwest. All summer long the empty blue sky glared at the brown fields and the burning sun pulled the last moisture from the soil. Rivers dwindled to trickles, streams became dry washes; winds knifed the topsoil loose and sent it soaring in clouds across the blasted land. The Spaniards, men of a cruel and ungenerous climate, knew the meaning of drought, and so did the Indians, whose ancestors had suffered through years and whole decades of rainlessness: the crops would fail, the cattle would grow lean, the people would make do on the stored surpluses of better years, and if things did not quickly grow better, they would soon become worse.

With the drought came the nomad raiders.

Wandering warriors had plagued the Pueblo folk for centuries. Apparently they came from the far north, for the language spoken by their descendants, the Navaho and the Apache, is closely related to the Athabascan group of languages spoken by the Indians of western Canada and Alaska. Archaeological evidence indicates that the nomads of the north may have begun raiding the Four Corners country as early as A.D. 800, and that they almost certainly played a part in bringing about the abandonment of that region by the Pueblos five centuries later.

By the year 1600 many bands of them roamed the territory east and north of the Rio Grande, preying on the Indians of the farming villages. They did not call themselves Navaho or Apache. Their name for themselves was *Diné,* "the People"—a word used as a tribal name by all Athabascan-speaking Indians. The pueblo-dwellers called them *apachu,* meaning "stranger" or "enemy." One band became known as *apachu nabahu,* "enemies of the cultivated fields." The Spaniards translated these names into "Apache" and "Navaho," and the names stuck so well that the Diné themselves have come to use them.

The invaders were not farmers. They were raiders, shrewd, aggressive, strong. They came from a cold land where there was no tradition of farming, because the earth would not readily yield crops; here in the Southwest, they lacked the patience to struggle against drought as the hard-working Pueblo farmers did. It was easier to let the Pueblos do the farming, and then to burst in and carry off the harvest.

Nor did they care to build permanent villages out of stone or adobe, in the Pueblo fashion. The Navaho and Apache felt no need to settle down. They had no wish to collect in groups of 500 or 1000 or more, and live jammed together in a town of tiny rooms. They liked privacy. They chose to travel in small family units, and to live in lonely dwellings placed at great distances from one another. The Navaho built circular domed houses called *hogans* out of logs and brush covered with mud; the Apache dwelling was a round hut of brush, the *wickiup*. Both nomad branches made crude pottery and fairly good baskets. They dressed in skins, and sometimes in garments woven of juniper fiber.

The Pueblo Indians occasionally suffered also at the hands of the other tribes of the great plains east of the Rio Grande —particularly the Comanche, sometimes the Kiowa or Shoshone. These people depended for their livelihood on hunting the immense herds of bison, but now and then swept through the pueblos to seize corn and other vegetables.

The drought that struck in 1660 affected the huntsmen and the nomads as much as it did the farmers. On the plains the grass died and the bison began a migration to more agreeable parts. Even the nuts and berries and roots with which the Indians of the plains bolstered their diets became scarce. Rather than search far and wide for food, the Apache and Comanche chose to raid the farming settlements to their west. Their old victims, the Pueblos, were sure to have storage bins full of corn; and the newcomers, the Spaniards, also were tempting targets, since their farms were stocked with cattle and sheep and pigs. The plains people were aware of the wealth of the Spaniards, for they had been doing business with them for some years: Apache and Comanche warriors would capture Indians from tribes farther to the east and sell them as slaves to the Spaniards of New Mexico, in return for horses, guns, and knives.

The first to feel the impact of the new cycle of nomad raids were the Piro-speaking pueblos southeast of the Rio Grande, where the rich salt deposits were found. On their west flank, these villages were separated from the river country by a line of mountains, while to the east the broad plains began, leaving them easily open to attack. They were handsome pueblos whose buildings were made of fine sandstone—rose-gray at Quarai, deep orange-red at Abó, a speckled gray-and-tan at Tabira, and so on along the line of towns to Taxique and Chilili in the northern part of the Piro zone. Christianity had taken a firm hold on these pueblos; their churches included the three largest in New Mexico.

All through the 1660's the Apache marauders plundered the Piro pueblos. As the dry summer uncoiled they attacked the quiet villages at harvest time and carried off the bulk of the corn, leaving the villagers barely enough to get through the winter, and some seed for next spring's crop. And next spring it was the same: the farmers labored against the drought to nourish their pitiful plants, and the Apache took a share of what little was produced. The townspeople attempted to defend themselves, but warfare was not natural to them, and they stood little chance against the fierce nomads. "The whole land is at war with the widespread heathen nations of Apache Indians, who kill all the Christian Indians they can find," declared a friar in 1669. "No road is safe; everyone travels at the risk of his life." If we can trust the friar's account, the sins of the Apache even included cannibalism. We are told that they attacked the pueblo of Taxique and carried captives into the plains: "There they build a great fire, near which they bind the person whom they have captured; they then dance around him, cutting off parts of his body, which they cook and eat, until they entirely consume him, cutting him to pieces alive."

The Spaniards, when they first took possession of New Mexico seventy years earlier, had sworn to defend the Pueblo folk against these very foes; it was the promise of Spanish military aid, more than anything else, that had induced the

Pueblo caciques to sign away their freedom to the white men. Now that aid was expected. But the Spaniards were hard put to meet their pledge. Since the colony had not flourished as hoped, its population in the 1660's was scarcely more than 2,500, and only a few of these were soldiers. The best that could be done by way of guarding the eastern frontier was to post little bands of soldiers at widely scattered outposts—five men here, five men there, five men farther along. These border patrols were of little value against the hordes of armed invaders. Requests went off to Mexico City for reinforcements, but the viceroy's officials did not seem to care much about the troubles of New Mexico, and provided excuses and delays instead of men.

The repeated raids, coupled with an apparently unending drought, brought the colony close to the starvation level. One company of Spanish border guards reported in 1668 that they had seen scores of Indians "lying dead along the roads, in the ravines, and in their huts." At one pueblo 450 people died of hunger. A friar wrote that there was "not a bushel and a half of corn or wheat in the whole kingdom." Nearly all the livestock was gone now, either dead of starvation or carried off by raiders, and both Spaniards and Indians were reduced to dining on leather; they took hides and even the straps from their carts, soaked and washed them, dusted them with corn meal, and roasted them in the fire, or ate them boiled with herbs and roots.

Disease followed upon famine. In 1671 an epidemic killed many people and most of the remaining cattle. The weakened settlers and Indians were powerless against the invaders from the plains, who now came even more frequently than before, since the drought was deepening and their own troubles were increased. The attacks became so merciless that the entire line of Piro villages was abandoned. No longer could the remaining Piros go through the grim struggle to scratch out a harvest, nor could they endure the furies of their enemies. The stone houses and the colossal churches were left to the wind and the weeds, and the Piros trekked westward across the mountains to the Rio Grande. There they scattered, some heading down past El Paso del Norte into northern Mexico, others taking refuge with their cousins in the southernmost river pueblos of Socorro and Senecú. But they found no security there. On January 23, 1675, an Apache war party came out of the mountains near Senecú and laid siege to the town. The pastor, Fray Alonso Gil de Avila, appeared in a window of the mission holding a crucifix and urging the people to have faith in God; an Apache arrow cut him down. More than half of the population of Senecú perished in the raid, and the rest escaped to Socorro. Senecú joined the roster of abandoned pueblos; no one ever lived there again.

It was a time of turmoil and terror, of unanswered prayers, of empty bellies and dry throats, of crumbling towns, of a disintegrating world. In the pueblos, the leaders of the secret societies met in the kivas to ask their gods to make the burden of existence easier to bear. In the churches, the Spaniards implored Jesus and the Virgin Mary and all the saints for help. The words spoken in the kivas and those whispered before the altar of Christ were different, but the things being said were the same. All over New Mexico, men were looking toward their gods and asking, How have we failed you? What must we do to atone? When will you cease to punish us? How much suffering must we endure?

6

Seeds of Revolt

As the Spanish settlers sought to understand the reasons for the calamities that had come upon their colony in the 1660's and early 1670's, they found themselves returning frequently to the theme of the long enmity between church and government. Had God shown His displeasure because of the way so many governors had worked to undermine the authority of the friars? About 1675, the Virgin Mary appeared in a vision to a dying girl and restored her to health, saying, "My child, go and tell everyone that the kingdom will soon be destroyed because of the lack of reverence shown to my priests. . . ." The miracle seemed both an omen and an order to mend ways. Terrified, the colonists asked one another if it might not be too late to win divine favor after all.

Governor Juan Francisco de Treviño took measures to end the feud between the two Majesties. Hereafter, the civil authorities would in no way hinder the attempts of the friars to exert control over the natives. The sly tactic of encouraging a revival of pagan rites would be abandoned forever, and the government would cooperate with the priests in keeping the Indians true to the Christian faith.

In fact, there had long since ceased to be any need for the governors to encourage Pueblo paganism. The period of troubled times that had begun in 1660 had seen the Indians desert their adopted creed by the thousands. The destruction of kivas and kachina masks in the purge of 1661 had helped to spur this process; persecution always stiffens the determination of an oppressed religious group. Then the disasters of the succeeding years—the worsening drought, the nomad raids, the famine, the epidemics—had left the Pueblos convinced that in accepting Christianity they had strayed from the right path. Plainly the god of the Christians had no real power, and only a return to the old way of the kachinas would save the Pueblos from utter calamity. In every village the traditional beliefs came back to life as these hard-pressed people returned to the ways of their ancestors.

The friars, of course, denounced this retreat into paganism, and, to demonstrate the new spirit of cooperation among Spaniards, Governor Treviño in 1675 took action to halt it. Reversing the decrees of some of his predecessors, he proclaimed total prohibition of the native rituals, which he termed "witchcraft" and "idolatry." He sent cavalry forces through the pueblos to arrest the leaders of the pagan revival. The heads of the secret societies, the medicine-men who performed the healing rites, the organizers of the kachina dances, were rounded up, forty-seven of them in all, and brought to Santa Fe to stand trial for the crimes of practicing sorcery and promoting idolatry.

The forty-seven were found guilty; witnesses were produced to testify that the accused men had been seen casting spells, and that was enough. Four, who were said to have tried to place an enchantment on a priest named Andrés Duran, were hanged in the plaza of Santa Fe. The others—the holiest men of the pueblos—received a public whipping, and were thrown into jail. There they remained for many weeks.

A kind of terror spread through the people of the Indian villages. They had tried the god of the white man, and that god had failed them, for he had brought nothing but hunger, drought, and slavery. Now all the forces of the spirit-world were loose in the land, spreading evil everywhere, and where were the medicine doctors who could protect the people against those dark powers? The doctors were in the white man's jail. The village people stood alone, defenseless, naked against the evil spirits. They could not perform the proper dances and rituals, not without their spiritual leaders, and the prayers they had learned from the white priests were worthless, so doom seemed inevitable.

There were anxious meetings in every pueblo, and then runners went from village to village carrying messages back and forth as the Indians sought to arrive at a policy that would let them present a unified front against their oppressors. They had never managed to unite before, but they had never been in such grave peril before, either. A policy emerged, and many of the pueblos backed it. At length a delegation of seventy Christian Indians from the Tewa villages went down to Santa Fe to demand the release of the imprisoned medicine doctors.

In true Pueblo style, the delegation did not offer a blustering free-them-or-else ultimatum. The Indians who called on Governor Treviño simply mentioned two possible consequences that might result from keeping the forty-three leaders in jail. If they were not freed soon, the visitors said, it might come to pass that every Indian in New Mexico would abandon his home and flee into Apache country, leaving the Spaniards masters of an empty realm. How would the Spaniards enjoy having to till their own fields and build their own houses and weave their own cloth? On the other hand, the delegates remarked, it was also possible that the continued imprisonment of the 43 would inspire the Indians of the province to rise in armed revolt and, striking with sudden ferocity, slaughter every Spaniard in New Mexico in a single day.

Thus the threats were stated—calmly, almost sadly, with no hint given of which course the Indians were likely to take. Would they meekly withdraw from their ancestral homes and force the Spaniards to shift for themselves? Or would they go on the warpath, launching a massacre against the aliens whom they outnumbered ten to one? Governor Treviño could not guess which; but he sensed the determination in his visitors' words, and chose not to find out what kind of retaliation they would offer. Backing away from the confrontation, he had the forty-three prisoners released and let them return to their pueblos.

Among those who had been flogged and imprisoned as a sorcerer was a certain medicine doctor named Popé, of the Tewa pueblo of San Juan, who would become a central figure in the dark events that lay ahead. He was a man of middle years—perhaps fifty or sixty—who had resisted Christianity all his life, clinging with fierce and bitter energy to the religion of the kiva. Often he had clashed with the Spaniards over his attempts to keep the traditional Indian faith alive; the friars regarded him as a dangerous trouble-maker, and there is evidence that he had been punished several times for his stubborn adherence to the kachinas.

Apparently Popé had suggested as early as 1668 or so that the time had come for the Pueblo folk to unite and drive the Spaniards from their land. His companions of the kiva nodded in agreement, but no one took these proposals of rebellion seriously, for, while the Indians by now all wished to be rid of the Spaniards, how could such a thing be accomplished? Large-scale warfare was a pastime the Pueblos had never engaged in; when they absolutely had to, they might go out and fight to drive raiders away from their villages, but the idea of taking the offensive, of initiating an attack, was foreign to them. Then, too, their advantage in numbers would be meaningless unless the many villages could agree to unite under a single leadership, or at least to follow a single plan of action. So long as the Keresan people were unwilling to make alliances with the Tewas, so long as Tanos were uneasy about Tiwas, what hope was there of crushing the true enemy of all the Pueblo tribes?

But after Popé emerged from the jail at Santa Fe, with the sting of the white man's lash still blazing on his back and the smell of the white man's dungeon in his nostrils, these objections no longer mattered. The Spaniards *must* be thrust from New Mexico, regardless of the obstacles in the way of achieving that goal. Consumed by hatred, possessed by a vision of his land restored to its old way of life, hungering for vengeance against those who had bruised his body and oppressed his spirit, Popé laid plans for revolt.

It was not something that could happen overnight. He saw that months or perhaps years of work would be needed in order to strike in the swift, coordinated way that was the Indians' only hope. So the old medicine doctor patiently built a web of alliances through the rest of 1675, and through 1676 and 1677 and the years that followed. He explained his dream of liberation to his trusted comrades in his own pueblo of San Juan first; then he began to seek allies in the other village. At the Keresan pueblo of Santo Domingo there was a man named Catiti who shared Popé's yearning for freedom; he was drawn into the scheme early, and drew others in. At the northern Tiwa village of Picuris, Popé found another strong supporter, a chieftain named Tupatú. At Taos, also a northern Tiwa village, Jaca conveyed Popé's ideas to the leaders of the pueblo. Slowly the number of conspirators grew. Excluded from the discussions was anyone who showed undue sympathy toward Christian teachings, or anyone who was peacefully inclined toward Spaniards in general.

The large pueblo of Taos became Popé's headquarters. He spent much of his time in one of the Taos kivas, communing with a mysterious figure said to be the spokesman of the Pueblo war god. The Indians described him as a black giant with fiery yellow eyes; he seems actually to have been a mulatto from Mexico, one Diego de Santiago, who had come to New Mexico as a servant to the Spaniards about fifty years before. Apparently he had married a woman of Taos and had taken up Indian ways, and now, in his old age, he lived in a kiva, practicing sorcery—an unseen, shadowy figure whom the Indians regarded as a supernatural being, practically a god. The black giant appears to have been a guiding figure of the revolt, counselling Popé on the best way of defeating the Spaniards. Popé let it be known that the war-god's spokesman had promised the Indians victory; he also revealed that three spirits of the underworld, named Caudi, Tilini, and Tleume, regularly entered the kiva through a passageway beneath its floor and gave him advice.

Rumors of these sinister events reached the Spaniards and contributed to their mood of uneasiness. They did not know that a revolt was being planned, but they were aware that the Indians were up to something in Taos, and that Popé was probably involved in it. But they dared not take action against him. The situation was too tense; the episode of the forty-three imprisoned medicine doctors had revealed their own weakness to them, and without definite proof of a conspiracy they feared to make any new arrests that might provoke the Indians into open hostilities. Perhaps the time of tension would pass, the Spaniards hoped; perhaps the rains would come again, the Apache raids would stop, the pueblos would enjoy happy harvests, and all would be well once more.

Into the troubled colony during this time came Fray Francisco de Ayeta, the new father-quartermaster of the Franciscan order in New Mexico. It was the duty of the father-quartermaster to see that the missions of the province under his jurisdiction were supplied with all things necessary to their welfare: food, clothes, livestock, money, tools, and so forth. Every three years the king's representatives in Mexico City set aside a charitable donation of goods for the friars in New Mexico, and the father-quartermaster would travel to the colony with the caravan of cargo.

Fray Francisco made his first such trip in 1674, leading the regular procession of wagons, mules, and oxen up the valley road during the summer. He was a robust old man, alert and energetic, who intended to labor with all his strength on behalf of the settlers of New Mexico, but who had no idea how bad things really were in the colony. As he proceeded northward, though, he began to discover the truth. It was then an arduous six-month journey for the wagon train from Mexico City to Santa Fe, and Fray Francisco paused briefly to rest at each of the Spanish haciendas he came to while following the river north. These were handsome estates, where isolated Spanish families lived like lords on large tracts of land, enjoying the attentions of servants and slaves. Yet each hacienda was walled and guarded. Here was the estate of Don Alonso García, the lieutenant-general of New Mexico, and here was Bernalillo, as the hacienda of the Gonzales Bernal family was known, and here was the estate of Captain Agustín de Carbajal, and at each of these pleasant country homes Fray Francisco heard the same stories: drought, discouragement, Apache raids, hunger, a sullen and explosive mood among the long-docile Pueblos. Many of the settlers seemed ready to give up and go back to Mexico, a thought that horrified the father-quartermaster, for if the province were to be abandoned, it must also then be lost to Christianity.

At Santa Fe the situation looked no better. The mountain capital—the only Spanish town in the province, except for the little outpost by the river at El Paso del Norte—was tense and restless. Signs of decay were everywhere. The great central plaza, which looked so impressive at first glance, seemed seedy and run-down. The adobe walls of the long, magnificent governor's palace that occupied the north side of the plaza were crumbling, and the main entrance was without doors. The church of Saint Francis on the plaza's east side seemed shabby, as did the barracks of the city's garrison, which faced it. That garrison—the capital's only regular defense force—consisted of just ten soldiers.

Beyond the plaza the cultivated fields began, and in each field was a settler's flat-topped, earth-colored adobe house. But the fields were dry and the crops were stunted. The faces of the settlers were bleak and grim. There was talk here, too, of admitting the failure of the New Mexico experiment and going elsewhere. Had Fray Francisco heard that the Apache had destroyed six Piro pueblos southeast of the river and one of the Zuni towns in the west? Was he aware that churches had been burned, and holy images mocked? Did he know that the Pueblos were turning away from Jesus to dance their satanic dances? What would happen next? How could the colony survive?

The father-quartermaster saw only one way of saving New Mexico. The Mexican government, which had shown only the coolest interest in the welfare of the colony far to its north, must be persuaded to send aid. He would call upon the viceroy, he promised, as soon as he reached Mexico City; he would ask for soldiers, horses, supplies, weapons; perhaps God would move the viceroy to be generous to New Mexico.

In the spring of 1676 Fray Francisco set out for Mexico City. He arrived in late summer, and, early in September, went before the viceroy's ministers to present his petition. He asked for fifty soldiers to guard the frontiers of New Mexico; a thousand horses; a dozen men to drive the horses; a six-month supply of food for the caravan; eight women to cook for the men en route to New Mexico; and some miscellaneous equipment. The total cost to the royal treasury, he estimated, would be 14,700 pesos—no small sum, but hardly a great investment when one considered that the survival of a province was at stake.

So eloquently did the father-quartermaster offer his plea that the viceroy took the unusual step of approving the request without waiting for permission from Spain. The necessary money was made available, and Fray Francisco was granted the right to accept enlistments. But who cared to fight for New Mexico? No one at all came forward. In despair the father-quartermaster went back to the viceroy, who told him he could have some convicted criminals as his soldiers, men who had been sentenced to serve the government, and thus were at the viceroy's disposal. From the jails of Mexico came forty-seven thieves and murderers to be defenders of New Mexico; at the last minute three men of somewhat better character signed up also, so Fray Francisco had his complement of fifty soldiers. On February 27, 1677, the father-quartermaster left Mexico, leading the convoy that he hoped would save the unhappy colony.

The northward trip was slow, taking nine months instead

of the expected six; much of the delay was caused by flooding on the Rio Grande, which held the party up interminably at El Paso del Norte. While they were camped at the pass, waiting for the river's flow to slacken, six of Fray Francisco's convicts fled, taking with them fifty-seven horses, three guns, and six saddles, and were never seen again. A seventh man had escaped a few weeks earlier.

Despite such mishaps, Fray Francisco remained optimistic. He crossed the river eventually and, as he marched toward Santa Fe, dropped off food, cattle, and goats at some of the afflicted settlements along the way. In November, 1677, he reached Santa Fe at last, and was greeted with joy and gratitude by the settlers and their new governor, Antonio de Otermín.

It seemed at first that the supplies the father-quartermaster had brought would carry the capital easily through any crisis that was to come: a hundred new arquebuses, a hundred hilts for swords and daggers, fifty saddles, fifty head of cattle, several hundred bushels of provisions, a thousand horses. Twenty of the newly recruited soldiers, outfitted with thick leather jackets and sturdy leather shields, were assigned to the defense of Santa Fe. But the moment of confidence swiftly fled. Had anything really changed? Would bushels of grain from Mexico be of any lasting value to a colony incapable of raising its own food? Would a few dozen surly soldiers give the settlers any real additional protection against the thousands of stony-faced Indians among whom they lived, and against the uncountable hordes of marauders on the frontier? So long as the drought continued, the colony's position would remain precarious. So long as a handful of troops held the responsibility for guarding more than 30 missions and keeping watch over dozens of pueblos, no Spaniard could feel safe in New Mexico. Fray Francisco realized that further aid was needed. By the beginning of 1679 the father-quartermaster was in Mexico City again, asking the viceroy for help.

Again Fray Francisco summoned his eloquence, reminding the viceroy of the hardships being suffered in New Mexico, of the century-long struggle to create a Spanish dominion there, of the valor and determination of the settlers, of the silent hostility of the Indians. He cited past royal decrees instructing the viceroy to take all necessary measures to insure the welfare of this outpost on the edge of his realm. The friar asked for more soldiers, more settlers, more supplies: "There can be no remedy," he said, "except to increase the number of people, so that everywhere, when the offender arrives, he will find the defender."

Specifically, the father-quartermaster wanted fifty soldiers to man the frontier posts and fifty to be stationed in Santa Fe. But this time the viceroy was unsympathetic. He had his own budget to look after; and, while Mexico was a wealthy land, he could not keep pouring good pesos into this obviously unsustainable northern colony. It was only three years since he had last provided charity for the wretched New Mexicans; were they serious about expecting more so soon? On May 16, 1679, the viceroy informed the father-quartermaster that his latest appeals had been found "not sufficiently convincing" and that the king would surely look upon further aid to New Mexico at this time as "a useless and unnecessary expense." The viceroy therefore declined to provide funds from the Mexican treasury for the defense of the colonists, although, if Fray Francisco wished, he would forward the request to Madrid for the king's consideration.

The father-quartermaster knew that it would take a year—or two, or three—for any kind of decision to come from the Spanish court. He could not wait. He resolved to go back to

New Mexico as quickly as possible, bringing with him only the regular charitable donation that the Mexican government made every third year to the northern missions. After spending the summer of 1679 purchasing and loading provisions and acquiring livestock, he departed for New Mexico on September 30, at the head of a caravan of twenty-eight wagons.

The slow, dreary journey brought him by the late spring of 1680 to Parral, the capital of New Biscay, as Mexico's northernmost province then was known. From there he sent word to Governor Otermín at Santa Fe that he had been unable to obtain military aid, but was on his way with food, equipment, and animals. He hoped to be at El Paso del Norte by August.

He kept that schedule. But in August the Rio Grande was running unusually high for the summer, and the wagon train could not cross: it was foolish to risk letting pigs or sheep, or even some of the wagons, be swept away by the turbulent waters. Fray Francisco made camp on the south bank and awaited a safer time. Shortly a detachment of horsemen appeared from the north and boldly rode across. It was a military escort, sent by Otermín to accompany the wagon train to Santa Fe: twenty-seven soldiers, commanded by an officer named Pedro de Leiva. But, though men on horseback could ford the river, wagons and livestock still could not, and Leiva and his troops settled in alongside Fray Francisco's caravan to wait until the water subsided. The mission of Our Lady of Guadalupe, in the tiny settlement south of the river, became their headquarters. They spent most of the month of August there.

Then, a little after dawn on August 25, 1680, two Indian messengers arrived at El Paso del Norte. Crossing the river, they went to the mission, and about eight o'clock were admitted to the room where Fray Francisco was staying. The couriers bore two letters for him.

One was from a settler named Juan Severino de Suballe, whose farm was located in southern New Mexico, near the present town of Belen. It was dated August 18 and addressed to Fray Diego de Mendoza, the pastor at the town of Socorro, to the south of Suballe's hacienda. The Indians of the pueblos, Suballe informed Fray Diego, had revolted. The Spanish settlements north of Sandía—near the modern city of Albuquerque—had been wiped out. Presumably Governor Otermín and everyone else up at Santa Fe were dead. Most of the outlying haciendas had been destroyed; the Carbajals were known to be dead, and so were Don Cristóbal de Anaya and all his family, but the people of the hacienda of Bernalillo had apparently been able to escape, and had joined the column of refugees now streaming down the Rio Grande Valley.

The second letter, dated August 20, was from Fray Diego de Mendoza at Socorro to Fray Francisco at El Paso del Norte. Here, Fray Diego told the father-quartermaster, is the terrible letter I have just received from Suballe. Presumably the survivors of the massacre would soon come pouring into Socorro, far below the zone of insurrection. Fray Diego asked for food for the refugees and soldiers to protect them, and suggested that troops be sent to Santa Fe "to see if all who are in the town have perished, for it is not right to leave them to their fate." A least four friars were known to have been murdered, Fray Diego added, and he wondered if any of the others were still alive.

The catastrophe that everyone had feared had come. The colony was shattered; if everything north of Sandía really was gone, then both governor and government had perished, and probably the representatives of the church as well. To Fray Francisco, the calamity meant the collapse of a sector of the Christian world, a victory for Satan. To Pedro de Leiva and his twenty-seven men the cause for grief was far less abstract, for they had left their families in the north, and knew nothing now of their fate. The scene at Our Lady of Guadalupe was chaotic. As Fray Francisco later declared, "The confusion . . . that has passed over my small forces since eight o'clock in the morning of the 25th could not be described on many reams of paper."

Two hours after the stunning news had come, though, some degree of order returned to the mission. The Spaniards at El Paso del Norte assembled for a council of war. General de Leiva read the two letters to the group, and called for a discussion of the action that should be taken. The men agreed quickly that they must cross the river and bring relief to the refugees who now were making their way by foot down the valley toward Socorro. After that, an expedition into the north would be necessary, to discover the state of things at Santa Fe and, if it were not too late, to rescue the residents of the beleaguered capital.

Fray Francisco pointed out that the colony now was leaderless; even if Governor Otermín and his officials had escaped the fury of the Indians, communications were disrupted and there was no way for the machinery of government to function. In the name of order and reason, he argued, the men at El Paso del Norte must hold an election and choose a provisional governor for the colony, someone in whom the absolute right to make decisions and give commands would be vested until normal conditions returned. Some of the soldiers grumbled at this. Evidently they were tempted by the notion of an end to government, an end to all givers of orders. Seeing the threat of anarchy in their murmured objections, Fray Francisco grew more firm: a provisional governor, he said bluntly, would be elected that afternoon.

The meeting next considered what should be done for the

relief of the victims. Fray Francisco quickly organized a plan. They must unload the wagons he had brought from Mexico, removing the tools and saddles and such things, and reload the wagons with emergency provisions for the refugees. Then they would have to get the wagon across the river somehow, along with two hundred head of cattle to be used for food. Pausing to rest only when absolutely necessary, they would get to the refugee camp with the greatest possible speed. The father-quartermaster's plan won immediate approval, and the meeting was adjourned.

Early in the afternoon came the sound of a drum and the blare of a military trumpet, calling the men together again for the election of a provisional governor. There was no contest. General de Leiva was elected unanimously; Fray Francisco led him to a chair, and each of the men swore allegiance to him. Then, the father-quartermaster wrote, Leiva was given "a baton of wood with a blue ribbon as a sign of his election as chief. After making very courteous responses and admitting himself to be the most unworthy member of the group, he received it, in the name of His Majesty, our king and lord, Charles II, whom God keep." Three volleys of shots were ceremonially fired in homage to the new governor.

Over the next three days, while the wagons were being unloaded and then reloaded with the emergency supplies, the plans for the relief expedition underwent some revisions. Leiva decided to make El Paso del Norte the main base for the refugees. The wagons would go out into New Mexico to bring them the emergency supplies, and then would carry them back across the river to safety. Meanwhile, as the slow-moving wagons were going forth, the soldiers would speed ahead up the river toward Santa Fe, telling any stragglers they met along the route to go to El Paso. If possible, they would liberate the capital, rescue its people, and suppress the revolt. If this could not be done, they would return with anyone they found to the camp at El Paso.

To Leiva's force of twenty-seven soldiers was hurriedly added fifty-one newly armed men—servants and grooms, mostly—recruited at El Paso. Each man was given an arquebus, two pounds of gunpowder, and a hundred bullets. There was not enough armor for the entire detachment, but most of the men had helmets and coats of mail, and eleven of the horses were armored.

Fray Francisco was not allowed to accompany the relief mission. Leiva told him to stay behind at El Paso, citing two reasons: the father-quartermaster was the man best able to look after the hundreds of refugees who would soon be crowding into Our Lady of Guadalupe, and, if the Indian rebellion should spread to the tribes around El Paso, a commanding figure like Fray Francisco would be needed to lead the defense of the mission. The father-quartermaster was displeased at being refused permission to enter New Mexico, but he had sworn to obey the provisional governor's orders, and he made no objections.

On August 30 the wagons began to roll and the soldiers rode out. "All are going absolutely raging," Fray Francisco wrote. "I believe under God that each one must be reckoned as ten men." By now, further fragmentary reports of the disaster had reached El Paso. Leiva had learned that he had lost not only all his property, but also his wife, three daughters, three sons, and eight grandchildren. Another officer had lost his mother and three sisters; a third, his wife and children. No man was untouched by the revolt. Their mission now was one of vengeance.

When they were gone, Fray Francisco and the other friars who had remained at the mission began the task of preparing for the influx of refugees. They slaughtered cattle and put the meat up to dry; they ground corn and made biscuits; and, when not stockpiling food, they made bullets. Days passed without word from the north. On September 8, finally, messengers came, bearing letters from Don Alonso García, the lieutenant-general of the colony, giving more details of the uprising than any of the previous messages to El Paso.

The northern pueblos, García wrote, had cast off Spanish rule all on the same day, obviously by prearrangement. Santa Fe had been attacked and burned. The pueblo churches had all been destroyed, and only eleven of the thirty-three missionaries had escaped; the Franciscan father-president had been killed at Santo Domingo. But not all the news was bad. Governor Otermín and many of the people of Santa Fe had survived, and were marching downriver. García himself had collected a second band of refugees from the haciendas south of Santa Fe, and now was waiting at a place called Fray Cristóbal for Otermín's party to arrive. When the two groups had joined, they would proceed together toward El Paso; but the need for food and clothing was urgent, and García hoped Fray Francisco's wagons soon would be reaching Fray Cristóbal.

It was something less than a total catastrophe, then. Yet there was no disguising the fundamental nature of what had happened. Rising in sudden wrath, the Pueblo folk had hurled the Spaniards out of New Mexico, bringing to an end eighty-two years of occupation. The colony was dead. The chances of its rebirth seemed slight. For Spain, for Christendom, the defeat was a stinging humiliation, an astonishing upheaval, a cause for sorrow and embarrassment, a shameful failure.

7

The Day of Reckoning

SPAIN had tasted such bitter reversals before. In 1565, after several false starts, Spaniards had succeeded in planting a colony in Florida, founding the town of St. Augustine. During the next twenty-five years, little Spanish outposts sprouted along much of Florida's Atlantic coast, and, beginning in 1593, Franciscan friars established a chain of missionary stations that brought Christianity to the Indians. But in 1597 a warlike Indian named Juanillo of the Guale tribe, angered because the friars had not wanted him to become the chief of his people, led a revolt in which a number of missionaries were slain and most of the missions north of St. Augustine were destroyed. The Spaniards struck back, however, defeating the rebels and disrupting their way of life so badly that starvation overtook them, and by 1600 their chiefs were flocking to St. Augustine to beg forgiveness. Restoration of the missions began in 1603, and within a few years the Spanish settlements in Florida were far stronger and more numerous than they had been before the uprising.

Another episode of this kind took place in northwestern Mexico in November, 1616. Here, in the Sierra Madre Mountains, the Spaniards exploited rich silver mines while Jesuit missionaries worked to make Christians out of the Tepehuan Indians, a simple agricultural tribe. The Jesuits denounced the religion of the Tepehuanes as "witchcraft," and clumsily attempted to suppress it, causing a Tepehuan prophet named Quautlatas to organize a holy war against them. Pretending to speak through a stone idol, Quautlatas urged his people to thrust all Spaniards out of their territory, and promised that anyone who died fighting the white man would magically return to life. A single well-coordinated attack took the lives of some four hundred Spaniards, including all but one of the Jesuits, and briefly broke Spanish control over the region. Two years of warfare followed; it took three military expeditions to subdue the rebels, and, though organized resistance ended with the death of Quautlatas and the other Indian leaders in 1618, it was not until 1623 that order returned to the Tepehuan district.

But the Tepehuan rebellion and the earlier insurrection in Florida were minor compared with what occurred in New Mexico. Those two uprisings had been confined to relatively small districts in which Spain had no great investment of men or energy, and successful Spanish counterattacks had been launched as soon as the first shock of defeat had faded. But New Mexico had been an entire vast province of the empire of Spain, thousands of square miles, on which almost a century and a half of effort had been expended. The Indians had not merely chased out a few dozen priests, or a few hundred miners; they had uprooted a sprawling settlement, with a capital city, dozens of outlying haciendas, and a far-flung network of missions. And, as the dazed and unbelieving survivors straggled toward safety in El Paso, it did not seem to anyone that it would ever be possible to recapture what had been lost. For the first time since Spain had begun to carve out her American empire in the late fifteenth century, the momentum of her advance had been emphatically checked. That was the shocking thing. Every Spaniard had confidently assumed that the empire would go on and on in constant expansion through the New World— suffering a small setback here and there, perhaps, losing a few lives to the Indians, but meeting no real opposition— and suddenly more than two thousand settlers had been flung from New Mexico, with the door, so to speak, slamming angrily shut behind them.

What had happened? How had the Indians—the peaceful, harmless Pueblos, of all people—managed to do this thing?

The story emerged gradually, over the weeks and months that followed the attack. The Spaniards put it together through a kind of detective work, questioning the survivors of the sudden onslaught and their own Indian servants—for not all the Pueblos had joined the conspiracy—and piecing together the muddled and often contradictory clues thus acquired. Much of what had taken place would never be known, for the victims could not speak and the victors kept no written accounts of their plot. Such history as there is of the event, then, has come to us mainly as a result of the Spanish inquiries, modified by old tribal traditions that anthropologists learned from the Indians in the nineteenth and twentieth centuries.

At the heart of the conspiracy was a man neither peaceful nor harmless: Popé, the embittered medicine doctor. We would call him a militant today, or perhaps a Pueblo nationalist. Certainly he was something of a religious fanatic, imbued with a fiery love for the kachina faith; but his initial and intuitive distaste for Christianity no doubt had been inflamed by the whippings and imprisonments he had received at the hands of the Spaniards, the worshippers of a supposedly loving god.

His resentment thus was partly abstract, partly personal. He loathed the Spaniards for what they had done to his land, and for what they had done to him. The conspiracy that he organized was basically political in nature—a union of tribes to break Spanish control over New Mexico—but it also had elements of a crusade, a holy war, and at the bottom of everything, perhaps, was Popé's purely private fury over the harsh treatment he had received. He was no saint. He was a man who sought the welfare of his people, but he also sought vengeance for wrongs he alone had suffered, and, as events revealed, he coveted power for its own sake—a trait completely uncharacteristic of Pueblo psychology.

In person he was a fierce and dynamic individual who took care to give the impression that he was in league with dark powers, and who inspired respect bordering on fear in those who dealt with him. As he built his conspiracy he cunningly exploited such links to the supernatural as the black giant who dwelled in the Taos kiva, and the three spirits of the underworld who, he said, advised him on matters of military strategy. He let it be known that demons and spirits attended him at all times; perhaps he believed it. In certain leaders greatness and madness are never very far apart, and Popé was such a leader.

With the help of his lieutenants—Catiti of Santo Domingo, Tupatú of Picuris, Jaca of Taos—he won pledges of support from nearly every pueblo. All of the Rio Grande villages joined the plot except the Piro-speaking towns around Socorro in the southern part of the valley; whether the Piros refused to take part or, for some reason, simply were not invited, is not clear. The other Pueblo groups varied in their enthusiasm for the uprising: the Tano-speaking towns were divided, some of them hesitating to make war against the Spaniards, others blazing with eagerness for revolt. A few of the Keres-speaking pueblos also were lukewarm about battle. The Tewas and northern Tiwas had the most belligerent attitudes; the Zuni and the far-off Hopi, who had barely felt the white man's impact, were nearly as avid to destroy him. Even in the pueblos where rebellious feelings ran highest, though, a few influential Christian chiefs spoke out against revolt.

By the summer of 1680, the alliance that had taken almost five years to weld was complete. Popé chose August 13 as the day of the uprising. The symbol of rebellion was a knotted cord; the knots were a code, announcing the number of days that remained before the day of reckoning. Swift runners brought the cords to the pueblos. At each village, smoke signals went up as a sign that the leaders understood the message, agreed with the date, and would be ready. Strict precautions were taken to prevent the plans from leaking; no one of doubtful loyalty was let in on the secret, and no woman in any village was told.

Even so, it proved impossible to keep the plot from the ears of those Indians who looked kindly on the Spaniards. One of those was Nicolas Bua, the governor of the Tewa pueblo at San Juan. This was Popé's own pueblo, and Bua was the husband of Popé's daughter. He had long been friendly with a number of Spaniards, and they had repaid his allegiance by helping him to become an important and wealthy man. Shortly before the scheduled date of the up-rising, Popé dramatically announced at a meeting of the San Juan plotters that he suspected his son-in-law of being a spy for the white men. At Popé's instigation, Bua was stoned to death in a cornfield the next day—an episode that was calculated to terrify any other would-be informers.

At the last moment several Indians did reveal the conspiracy. On August 9, men of two Tano pueblos—San Lázaro and San Cristóbal—told their priest that there would be a general revolt four days hence. At Pecos an Indian newly converted to Christianity, making his confession to his priest, admitted the same thing. On the afternoon of August 9 the Indian governors of the pueblos of Taos and Tesuque arrived at Governor Otermín's palace to tell him that an attack was imminent. They "now regarded the Spaniards as their brothers," they said, and had declined the invitation to join the revolt. Otermín was not overly alarmed—there had been rumors of a revolt many times during the past few years, but nothing had ever happened—yet, just for the sake of caution, he relayed the story to the haciendas south of Santa Fe, and to the outlying missions. In the event of trouble, Otermín advised, colonists in the south should gather for mutual defense at the town of Isleta, and those in the north should assemble at the capital.

The warnings came too late. Popé, learning that the secret was out, sent word to his confederates that they should strike on August 10, not the 13th. Possibly August 10 had been the real date all along, a fact known only to the inner circle of conspirators, and the August 13 date had been selected to confuse the Spaniards to whom certain traitors were likely to reveal it. In any event, at sunrise on Saturday the 10th the Indians of New Mexico launched their assault against the almost totally unprepared Spanish settlers.

The first news of catastrophe reached Otermín at seven o'clock on Saturday morning, as he was on his way to church. Wild-eyed, panicky, a soldier named Pedro Hidalgo galloped into the plaza of Santa Fe and cried out that the

Indians of Tesuque, just nine miles north of the capital, had rebelled. Painting themselves with the garish colors of war, they had gone into their church at dawn and murdered the priest at his altar. "What is this, children?" the friar cried, as the first blows were struck. "Are you mad? Don't get excited—I will help you and die a thousand deaths for you." But one death was enough; the priest fell, and the Indians set fire to the church, after ripping down and destroying all the holy images it contained. Also murdered was a white trader who lived at the pueblo.

Otermín sent a squad of soldiers to Tesuque to see what had occurred there and to quell any disturbance. They came back later in the day with word that the priest and the trader were indeed dead, the church had been wrecked, and the Indians had seized all the horses and cattle belonging to the mission. Nor had the troops been able to stop the upheaval, because the whole countryside was at war. The pastors of the pueblos of San Ildefonso and Nambé had also been murdered; flames could be seen over the church at San Juan; most of the isolated farms of the district had been overrun. The whole family of General Pedro de Leiva was dead; Doña Petronila de Salas with her ten sons and daughters had been murdered; thirty-eight people had been slain at the hacienda of Thomé Dominguez de Mendoza. Bands of armed Indians were moving grimly through the hills.

Everyone who was still alive on the outskirts of Santa Fe hurried into the city, and the gates were locked. Otermín distributed weapons to those able to use them. More than a thousand men, women, and children huddled in terror in the capital, along with their farm animals and horses; a garrison of 150 men, less than half of them trained soldiers, guarded the frightened city. All day Saturday and on into Sunday messengers from distant outposts arrived, bringing tales of death and destruction, burning churches, murdered friars. Pecos and Taos had joined the revolt; Santa Clara, San Cristóbal, Santa Cruz, Picuris, San Marcos, and all the other pueblos around Santa Fe had risen; the friars' capital at Santo Domingo was in Indian hands; the whole land had gone mad. No news came from southern New Mexico at all. Were they dead down there too, in Isleta and Socorro? Where was Alonso García, the lieutenant-general of the province? Who would come to the aid of Santa Fe?

In the western pueblos, far from the bloody Rio Grande, the rebellion had been completely effective. Ácoma had killed its priest and regained the independence it had lost in such a frightful way in 1599. There was one missionary to serve the Zuni pueblos; he was killed. The four priests in the Hopi villages died.

The Hopi pueblo of Oraibi has preserved a traditional account of its participation in the revolt. The leaders of the uprising there all disguised themselves in kachina masks, with the two strongest men, Haneeya and Chavayo, wearing the mask of the kachina known as the Warrior. At dawn, one man made the sound of a screech-owl as the signal to attack. Following their kachina-masked leaders, the Hopi men rushed to the church; Chavayo killed the Spanish soldier who guarded the entrance, and they burst inside. While some of the Hopi fought with the other Spanish troops, a few smashed holes in the roof of the priests' quarters, and finally Haneeya dropped through the ceiling to slay the friars, José de Espeleta and Agustín de Santa Maria. The bodies of the two priests were carried down the mesa and buried at its base under a mound of rocks. The church bells and the vessels used in the mass were sealed in a cave, along with the swords and armor of the dead soldiers. The soldiers' spears were given to the One Horn Society, one of the many Hopi secret societies;

it is said that the One Horn priests at Oraibi still have them. The church was demolished down to its last stone, and its great beams were used in the kivas. The sheep and cattle of the mission were divided among the people. It was the same, apparently, at the other Hopi villages: Fray José de Figueroa, the priest at Awatovi, and Fray José de Trujillo, who was at Shongopovi, also perished, and their churches were obliterated.

The colonists penned up in Santa Fe spent an uneasy weekend. On Monday, August 12, lookouts posted on the rooftops gave the alarm that everyone had feared: bands of Indians could be seen moving toward the city. The next morning there were at least five hundred of them, camped in the cornfields just south of Santa Fe. Some were on horseback, most on foot; all were painted in bizarre and frightening patterns. Many of them were wearing Spanish armor that they had stripped from the dead, and carried Spanish spears, swords, or guns. Taking possession of the laborers' huts on the outskirts of town, the Indians shouted whoops of defiance and performed frenzied little dances of triumph. Santa Fe was under siege.

The invading force consisted of Tanos from the pueblos east of the Rio Grande, and some Towas from Pecos. Otermín ordered Santa Fe's two brass cannons trained on them, and then attempted to parley, inviting one of the Indian leaders to enter the city under a pledge of safe conduct for negotiations. The Indian, known to the Spaniards as Juan, was an intelligent, able man, who had spent much time among the Spaniards, spoke their language well, and seemingly had accepted Christianity gladly. He agreed to confer with Otermín. The governer, citing Juan's past record of loyalty to the Spaniards, asked him how he could be a leader of the rebels now. Had he gone insane? But Juan ignored the question. He had brought with him two crosses, one white, one red. Holding them both toward Otermín, he asked the governor to select one. "If you choose the white," he said, "there will be no war, but you must all leave the country. If you choose the red, you must all die, for we are many and you are few. Having killed so many Spaniards and priests, we will kill all the rest."

Still thinking he could reason with the man, Otermín chided Juan for falling away from Christianity, and dangled the hope of a full pardon for the rebels if they would return quietly to their homes and resume obedience. Juan said he would discuss this with his companions, and went back to the Indian camp. After a while he entered Santa Fe again, to propose various terms under which the Indians would consider ending the hostilities. The terms were unacceptable to Otermín, who realized that Juan was merely toying with him while waiting for reinforcements to arrive. The governor said brusquely that if the Indians did not withdraw immediately, the Santa Fe garrison would come forth to disperse them.

Juan carried this threat to the others, and the Indians at once began their attack, advancing on the city with howls of rage. Otermín sent a force out to meet them. The battle lasted all day, with the governor himself leading it much of the time. By setting fire to the houses in the cornfields, the Spaniards succeeded in driving the Indians back into the foothills of the mountains, and might have scattered them altogether. But as night fell, a thousand new Indian warriors suddenly appeared—Tewa reinforcements from San Juan, Santa Clara, and San Ildefonso, and a force of Tiwas from Taos. In the face of such a threat Otermín could not leave the women and children unguarded, and he was compelled to withdraw into the city, leaving the Indians in command of its outskirts. The day's skirmish had cost one Spanish life, and fifteen men had been wounded; the Indian casualties had been much heavier.

During the night more Indians appeared. Now some 2500 of them surrounded Santa Fe; Popé and Catiti were among them. The opportunity to break through the Pueblo ring and escape from the capital was lost now: the Spaniards could do nothing but wait. There was no action on August 14 or 15. On the morning of the 16th, the Indians made their move, swarming through Santa Fe's suburbs and occupying most of the town. The Spaniards, barricaded in the heart of the city, controlled little more than the plaza and the buildings around it. In the course of that day's fighting the Indians cut the ditch that supplied the capital with water; Otermín sent troops out to retake and repair the ditch, but they could not reach it, and were driven back behind the gates of the plaza.

An Indian attempt to set fire to the church of Saint Francis on the east side of the plaza failed. At noon, though, the Indians rushed up to the walls of the governor's palace itself, where most of the settlers had taken refuge, and tried to burn it, hurling torches at the chapel at one end of the palace. The entire garrison fought to save the chapel, and managed to save it after a struggle that lasted all afternoon. But the Spaniards came under heavy fire from the stolen guns in the hands of the Indians, and scarcely a man went unwounded.

At nightfall on August 16 the Indians withdrew, leaving the settlers still in control of the capital's center. The food and ammunition of the weary defenders were beginning to run low, now, and that night the first miseries of thirst struck the waterless city. In the morning the onslaught began again. The Indians hurled stones into the plaza, raked it with arrows fired from the high ground across the way, and peppered the Spaniards with gunshots from their arquebuses. By way of shattering Spanish morale they shouted that they had made an alliance with the Apache, who were coming to join the seige. Several times that day the Spaniards rushed from behind their fortifications to make desperate and unsuccessful attempts to recapture the water ditch. In one of these sorties Governor Otermín was wounded—hit twice in the face by arrows and once in the chest by an arquebus shot—but he remained on his feet and continued to direct the troops.

Toward the close of the day the Indians captured the two cannons that defended the ends of the plaza. Facing the possibility of bombardment by their own artillery pieces, the Spaniards frantically charged, seized the cannons, and dragged them behind their own lines. Jeering, screaming Pueblos closed in on the embattled plaza as night fell. Unable to break through into the governor's palace, they contented themselves with setting fire to the church and the adjoining buildings on the plaza, and to the houses beyond them. "The whole town became a torch," one witness wrote. Through the haze of smoke and flame came strangely familiar sounds: as a bitter jest the Indians were singing the Latin words of the Catholic liturgy.

After a terrible night of parched throats and fear-tightened nerves, the Spaniards resolved to make one last attempt, on the morning of Sunday, August 18, to break the siege. The farm animals that were crammed into the palace along with the thousand settlers had begun to die of thirst, and the threat of disease now had to be added to those of starvation and lack of water. After attending mass, Otermín and his hundred-odd soldiers burst from the palace and flung themselves frenziedly into the cordon of Indians. The sudden charge shook the confidence of the besiegers, and after some fierce fighting the Indians began to drop back. The Spaniards, buoyed by a kind of wild ultimate energy, forced their enemies through the streets of the ruined capital until, giving way to contagious panic, the Indians abruptly broke and ran. When the fighting ended, three hundred of the attackers were dead and forty-seven more were prisoners of the Spaniards.

The water ditch was repaired and the settlers and their animals slaked their thirst. The siege of Santa Fe had been broken, after five awful days. But what future was there for its people? Their buildings now were charred, roofless hulks. Their fields had been laid waste. They had no reserves of food. They had been granted a miraculous deliverance this time, but the Indians might return in a day or a week, and how could they be driven off again? Questioning the 47 captives, Otermín learned that the Pueblo gods had decreed the death of every male Spaniard in New Mexico; the prisoners claimed that this sentence had already been carried out in the entire district from Taos to Isleta, the Santa Fe people alone still surviving.

The situation in the north seemed hopeless. After conferring with his lieutenants and the clergymen, Otermín decided to abandon the capital and lead the settlers downriver to Isleta, where, he assumed, the colonists of the south had gathered under the command of Don Alonso García. At least the survivors would be united that way, and together might be able to devise some plan for the restoration of the province. Accordingly, Otermín had the forty-seven Indian prisoners executed, and on August 21 the awful exodus from Santa Fe began. The colonists left, Otermín declared, "without a crust of bread or a grain of wheat or maize, and with no other provision for the convoy of so many people except four hundred animals and two carts belonging to private persons, and, for food, a few sheep, goats, and cows."

The sour smell of burned buildings oppressed them as they

left. A dismal pall of ashes hung in the air. There were only enough horses to bear the sick and the wounded; the others went on foot, carrying their possessions on their backs. Stunned, shaken, the colonists stumbled through the debris that choked their city and started down the sloping rock-bound countryside that led to the Rio Grande. Over their heads as they marched fluttered the century-old flag of yellow silk that Don Juan de Oñate had carried, so unimaginably long ago, on his triumphal entry into the newly founded colony of New Mexico.

Indians were camped on the hills flanking the valley. The colonists, plodding southward, saw the smoke signals rising, saw the little groups of watching warriors, and, trembling, tried to hurry the pace of the march. But it could not be hurried. It was a trek of the old, the feeble, the very young; despite the menace of the Indians in the hills, despite the bite of hunger, despite the remorseless summer heat, the refugees were forced to advance at the pace of the slowest among them.

The Indians did not attack. Perhaps they felt that the withdrawal of the Spaniards from their land was sufficient; possibly they had some thought of waiting until the hardships of the exodus made the marchers easy prey. Whatever the reason, the settlers were unmolested. They could not understand that. Nor could they understand it when they came to Santo Domingo, the seat of the church headquarters: they found three dead friars here, and five other Spaniards who had died defending the priests, but—contrary to rumor—the church was unharmed, and the silver chalice, the lamps, the vessels for incense, and all the other implements of the holy service were sitting in their customary places. Why this curious show of reverence?

It was not the same farther downriver. Haciendas had been

wrecked and their owners brutally slaughtered, even women and children; and the tokens of Christianity had been uprooted. At the pueblo of Sandía, the interior of the church was a ruin, everything smashed and desecrated, the carved figures of the saints hacked to pieces; an attempt at setting fire to the building had succeeded only in part, though. Near one hacienda the refugees were joined by a friendly Indian who had broken away from the rebels. Otermín asked him why the revolt had happened, and the Indian said it was because the people were "tired of the work they had to do for the Spaniards and the clergy," who "did not allow them to plant, to do other things for their own needs; and that being weary they had rebelled."

Continuing southward, looking for some place that had not been destroyed, where they might hope to find food and lodging and safety, the colonists several times found themselves beset by small Indian war parties, and managed to drive them away. Near the ruined hacienda of the Carbajal family they encountered another friendly Indian, a man more than eighty years old, and again Otermín asked questions about the revolt. Why had it begun? Because, the old man said, the Spaniards had tried to take away from the Indians the ways of their ancestors, the faith by which they have lived and thrived. How long had the villagers been planning the uprising? Twelve years, said the Indian; maybe longer. Were any Spaniards still alive in the southern half of the province? Yes, the old man declared: many of them had assembled at Isleta after the fighting began. But they were no longer there, he told Otermín; they had gathered up everything they could carry and gone off somewhere down the valley.

That was somber news; Otermín and those who marched with him had counted heavily on resting and replenishing their strength at Isleta. But when they reached the town on

August 27, they found that the old Indian had told the truth. The place was deserted. Where was Lieutenant-General García? Where were all those in his charge? The governor sent four soldiers ahead to find him and to order him to stop until the Santa Fe refugees could catch up.

The soldiers went down into the desert country south of the last inhabited pueblo, Socorro, and found García and the southern group of refugees camped at an outpost known as Fray Cristóbal. The lieutenant-general readily agreed to ride back with them and discuss the situation with Otermín. On September 6, García reported to the governor, who by this time had led his band of marchers almost to Socorro. It was not a happy reunion: the moment García rode into the camp of bedraggled, gaunt outcasts from Santa Fe, Otermín told him he was under arrest, and, despite the seriousness of the Spaniards' predicament, an elaborate trial now began, complete with all the finicky legal procedure of a formal Spanish courtroom.

García was accused of insubordination. Otermín had asked him to come to the aid of besieged Santa Fe; he had not come. Then Otermín had told him to wait at Isleta for the northern refugees; instead, on his own authority, he had gone south with the settlers under his command. García, apparently expecting trouble of this sort, had brought a sheaf of affidavits and depositions to prove his good faith. He claimed that he had never received Otermín's messages; hearing of trouble in the north, he had tried to get messengers of his own through to the capital, but they had been unable to enter the region of the disturbance. Then stragglers reaching Isleta had brought word that everybody in the north was dead and all settlements had been destroyed. The logical thing to do, García had decided, was to save those who still lived by evacuating southern New Mexico before the rebels reached it, and so he had begun to march downriver.

For most of that day of September 6 the debate continued; Otermín, basically a reasonable man, finally saw that García's story was plausible, and cleared him of the charges. Orders were given to resume the march. As the Santa Fe people readied themselves to move on toward Fray Cristóbal, though, a worrisome cloud of dust appeared on the southern horizon. Indian warriors? No. It was the advance party from El Paso del Norte, some forty mounted soldiers under General Pedro de Leiva. Leiva, who had been elected New Mexico's provisional governor at El Paso, gave up that office upon discovering that Governor Otermín was still alive, and a happy celebration followed.

The three groups went on together to Fray Cristóbal, arriving on September 13. Conditions there were bleak: some two thousand homeless people, with scarcely any food, were gathered in a wretched dusty place incapable of supporting more than a few dozen souls. They could not stay there; they could not go back to Santa Fe; the only remaining choice was to proceed to El Paso del Norte, where the father-quartermaster, Fray Francisco de Ayeta, was waiting to give aid to the victims of the catastrophe. But that meant abandoning New Mexico, probably for good.

There was hardly scope for much discussion of alternatives. The column of refugees, after a brief halt at Fray Cristóbal, straggled on down the river on the dreary trek to El Paso del Norte. By the beginning of October everyone was camped on the north bank of the Rio Grande; the wagonloads of emergency supplies sent by Fray Francisco had sustained them satisfactorily, if not abundantly, through this phase of the sad journey. Then came the strenuous business of fording the river. Fray Francisco, watching the refugees totter into the mission of Our Lady of Guadalupe south of the river, said he had never seen "such great unhappiness and pitiful tragedy, with the need corresponding to the great numbers, and the poor women and children on foot and unshod, of such a hue that they looked like the dead."

By October 9, the survivors of what had been the Spanish colony in New Mexico were living in three camps surrounding the mission. Fray Francisco and other friars went among the bedraggled settlers offering prayers and consolations, and distributing the food and clothing the father-quartermaster had brought with him from Mexico that summer. A census of the refugees showed that 1,946 Spaniards had reached El Paso safely, out of nearly 2,500 who had lived in New Mexico prior to the morning of August 10. Close to 400 colonists had died in the uprising; the other 150 or so who were missing had slipped into Mexico on their own, without joining either of the two main groups of refugees, and now were facing an uncertain fate as they tried to reach the Mexican settlements beyond the wastelands.

What would happen to the New Mexico colony now? For the time being, everyone would remain at El Paso del Norte. An improvised town quickly took shape there, made of huts which Fray Francisco described as "built in an orderly manner, each one living in the house which he has made with his own hands of sticks and branches." That would do temporarily. But when everyone had recovered from the privations of the exodus, what then?

A few soldiers argued in favor of an immediate attempt to reconquer New Mexico. But such a scheme hardly seemed likely to succeed, at least not yet, and it received no serious consideration. A much larger faction of the settlers wanted to turn their backs on New Mexico altogether, and keep on heading south, into the far wealthier, more peaceful land of

Mexico, from which their ancestors had come over the past four generations. That would mean, though, the permanent abandonment of a district that once had been part of the Spanish realm, an idea intolerable to the leaders of the refugees.

Fray Francisco, while waiting for the refugees to reach El Paso del Norte, had already realized that the colonists would probably want to abandon the province, and, lest it be lost to Christianity forever, had quietly taken a cunning step to prevent them from quitting it. Once the settlers crossed the Rio Grande at El Paso, the father-quartermaster had reasoned, they would no longer be under the jurisdiction of Governor Otermín of New Mexico because a different province, that of New Biscay, began just south of the river. (A similar situation prevails today. North of the river lies the city of El Paso, Texas, in the United States of America. The place where the refugees had camped, south of the river, is now part of the city of Juárez in the Mexican state of Chihuahua.) In order for the refugees to travel any distance into Mexico, they would have to get permission from the governor of New Biscay to cross the territory under his control.

Therefore Fray Francisco wrote to the governor of New Biscay, explaining the situation and asking him to refuse such permission if the colonists requested it. The governor agreed. With the backing of his superior, the Mexican viceroy, he ruled that those who had fled from New Mexico could not cross or even enter New Biscay. Rather, they would have to remain camped at El Paso del Norte until such time as it was possible for them to return to their own province. Although El Paso del Norte, technically, was part of New Biscay, the governor declared that he would temporarily consider it an extension of New Mexico. This allowed

Governor Otermín to retain authority over his people during their sojourn in exile.

When talk of settling in Mexico began to circulate among the refugees, then, Fray Francisco produced his correspondence with the governor of New Biscay. The colony, he said, would not be allowed to disintegrate. Everyone must remain at El Paso until New Mexico could be reoccupied, and those who disobeyed would be charged with treason against the king, an offense punishable by death.

The colonists understood. There would be no ease for them until they had regained New Mexico for Jesus and for their country. With that point driven home, Fray Francisco departed for Mexico City, arriving in January, 1681, to apply for the soldiers and arms that would be needed for the reconquest.

8

New Mexico Under Popé

WONDERSTRUCK, the Pueblo folk were tasting the sweetness of their victory.

The Spaniards were gone. They actually were gone. A people who had grown accustomed to defeat, who had suffered at the hands of fiercer tribes for centuries, had in one glorious convulsion of wrath expelled from their midst the strangers who had come with guns and horses and armor to conquer them, the white men who had convinced half a world of their invincibility. Mexico still labored under the Spanish lash; Peru, the realm of the Incas, had entered its second century of miserable slavery; yet in New Mexico the meek farmers of the mud villages had triumphed. Here were Spanish bones to prove it; here were the tableware and linens they had left behind in their flight; here were the ashes of their capital city.

Popé ruled in New Mexico now.

Obliterating all traces of Christianity was his first goal. "The god of the Christians is dead," Popé proclaimed. "He was made of rotten wood." Those churches that had not been destroyed in the uprising were torn down now, so that nothing was left of them. Bonfires consumed the great wooden crosses that had marked each pueblo's conversion. Images of Jesus, Mary, and the saints were gleefully fed to the flames. At every village ceremonies of debaptism were held, in which the Indians were scrubbed clean of the taint of Christianity by water and the suds of the yucca plant. Henceforth it was forbidden to use the Christian names the priests had bestowed; there would be no more Josés and Marias and Jesuses in the pueblos. Nor was anyone permitted to speak a word of Spanish. Whatever the white man had brought to the land must be rooted out.

Not even the plants introduced by the Spaniards could be cultivated now. Watermelons, peaches, onions, wheat, the grapes from which the priests had made their sacramental wine, all were banned. Chili peppers, apples, plums, lemons, oranges—Popé had them ripped up, cast away. Only the old crops remained: corn, squash, beans. The same with the white man's animals: the pigs and sheep of the colonists were slaughtered, and the horses were set free from the corrals. (They were promptly captured by the warlike Indians of the plains, and an entire civilization was thereby transformed. The reckless, hard-riding Sioux and Kiowas and Shoshone and Cheyenne who thundered across the plains until the nineteenth century rode steeds that were descended, for the most part, from those let loose in New Mexico in 1680.)

The old kivas were reopened and new ones were constructed. Kachina masks were fashioned to replace those that the friars had taken away. The eradication of the Spaniards' imprint was accompanied by a frenzied religious revival, marked by wild dances, processions, offerings to the old gods, joyous and intense reaffirmations of the long-suppressed faith. According to reports that reached Fray Francisco de Ayeta within a few months of the revolt, the Pueblos had so enthusiastically returned to what the father-quartermaster called "the worship of Satan" that "not a sign has been visible of their ever having been Christians."

Time had been made to turn backward in its course. Briefly, for the Indians of New Mexico, it seemed as if the last hundred years had been blotted out, and all would again be as it had been before the Spaniards ever came.

But time never can be made to turn back. The changes wrought by the Spaniards were not so easily undone. Churches could be burned, grapevines pulled apart, yet certain Spanish ideas continued to infect the pueblo country, and, curiously, it was the reactionary Popé who kept those ideas alive.

Even while trying to wipe away all traces of the Spaniards, Popé tried to cling to the most alien concept they had brought: the notion that the once-independent villages should be ruled by a central authority, by a supreme governor. He would be that governor, of course. He took up residence in Santa Fe, moving into the adobe palace so lately occupied by Governor Otermín. Donning a fantastic outfit of gaudy-hued robes, and wearing a bull's horn on his forehead as a symbol of his power, Popé strutted and capered through the white man's capital, demanding that his subjects bow to him precisely as though he had succeeded to Otermín's rank and grandeur. Sometimes he even climbed into Otermín's old carriage of state and had himself drawn through the streets of the city. Indians who had not taken up arms against the Spaniards—or who had dared to disobey Popé's whims—were enslaved and used as servants. Just as in the days of the Spaniards, decrees went forth from Santa Fe, and the people of the outlying pueblos were expected to heed them. The central government continued to demand tribute from the villages, and, when Popé toured his kingdom, he insisted on being received at every pueblo with the show of honors once bestowed on the Spanish governor and on the father-president of the church.

The Pueblos had never really been a unified people, of course, but Popé's ill-advised attempt to weld them into a single nation succeeded only in driving the tribes farther apart than they had ever been before. By what right, the Keres and Tiwa people asked, does this Tewa try to rule over us? Why, wondered the people of Pecos, should we take orders from a man of Caypa? As Popé's reign became increasingly oppressive, the fragile unity that had allowed the Pueblos to overthrow their conquerors was shattered beyond repair. The Indian despot in Santa Fe had begun jailing or even executing his political foes, and was levying crushing tributes against the villages that opposed his rule. The new masters of the Pueblo country all seemed to be Tewas and Tanos, and soon the Keres, Towa, and Tiwa people were in rebellion against them. To some it seemed that things had been better under the Spaniards than they were under the harsh rule of Popé. Civil war split the land. It grew dangerous to travel outside one's own pueblo; bands of warriors roamed the countryside between, raiding fields and sometimes attacking villages; some towns were burned and had to be abandoned. Even in the ruling group there was dissension: the Tanos, quickly wearying of Popé's tyranny, talked of deposing him and making Tupatú, of the Tano pueblo of Picuris, chief in his place.

During this time of turmoil the drought continued with scarcely a break. Harvests were slender, both because of the dry weather and because farming chores had been neglected for the sake of making war. The Apache, too, renewed their assaults on the outlying villages. An entire group of Tano pueblos in the Galisteo region east of the Rio Grande was depopulated as a result of these raids; the homeless Tanos scattered, some going to live with other Tanos closer to the river, some moving into a Tewa settlement, others taking over the deserted Spanish houses in Santa Fe.

Things had not returned, then, to the happy state of the era before the coming of the Spaniards. Popé had learned, from the white men whom he hated, such things as the lust for power and the joys of oppression, and in his effort to organize the people of the Rio Grande into an imitation of a centralized European state he wrecked all hope of reviving the old orderly Pueblo life. He succeeded only in inflaming tribal tensions and in wasting the energies of his countrymen on foolish quarreling. By casting out the Spaniards, the Indians found, they had merely replaced a rational tyrant with an irrational one.

While the wild early excitement of liberation was crumbling into this somber reality of disillusionment for the Pueblos, the Spaniards were planning their campaign of reconquest. Fray Francisco de Ayeta, when he reached the court of the viceroy in Mexico City early in 1681, was shown a royal order that had recently arrived from Madrid: do everything possible to prevent the loss of New Mexico, the king commanded. His decree was not a direct response to the Pueblo revolt, for it was dated June 25, 1680, almost two months before the outbreak of that revolt. What it was, in fact, was a reply to Fray Francisco's plea for help of May, 1679. Functioning at its usual pace, the Spanish government had finally deigned to let the Mexican viceroy know that it did not want New Mexico abandoned. It was too late for that; but the viceroy, having learned the king's wishes, was now willing to provide military aid to the wretched colonists.

Fray Francisco himself received the viceroy's commendation "for the kindness and promptness with which he has acted in order to maintain and save the said people," and was informed that he need no longer concern himself with their plight: the Franciscan order had named him father-quarter-master for the entire western hemisphere, and wished him to return to Spain to discuss his new duties. However, as the plans for reconquest developed, it became clear to everyone that the indomitable figure of Fray Francisco was vital to the morale of the people of New Mexico, and the viceroy asked him to delay accepting his promotion in order to accompany the wagon train back to El Paso. The father-quartermaster replied that he would gladly do this, even if this loyalty to the colonists should cost him his new office.

By September, 1681, Fray Francisco was back in El Paso, having brought the colonists weapons, provisions, and some new soldiers. The reconquest could now begin, he announced. Governor Otermín, though, was lukewarm about the scheme. He had seen how the Indians fought, and had little enthusiasm for sampling their fury again. Nor did he believe that the troops at his disposal were capable of winning; they were poorly trained and ill-equipped, and most of them shared his lack of confidence in the success of the project. Nevertheless, the king and the viceroy commanded Otermín to undertake the reconquest, and, whatever his private hesitations, he would not shirk his duty to his monarch.

Only the friars seemed to think the plan would work. They felt that the Indians, after a year of devil-worship, would be eager to live Christian lives again, and would seek pardon for what they had done the moment the Spaniards reappeared. On the other hand, certain influential men of the colony refused to take part in the reconquest at all. El Paso had begun to seem quite attractive to them; it was safe and quiet, and they had started to rebuild their herds of cattle, with the chance of making a good profit by selling surplus animals to the settlers in New Biscay. Why go back to the land of such woe? Why risk another defeat? It was necessary for Otermín to threaten legal action against these men before they would cooperate.

On November 5, 1681, he finally began his march into New Mexico. His army consisted of 146 Spaniards—many of them hardly more than boys—and 112 warriors from friendly Indian tribes, plus twenty-eight servants and four or five friars, including Fray Francisco de Ayeta. The expedition was equipped with 975 horses and a number of oxen and mules to pull the baggage carts.

They traveled north by the familiar river route, and on November 26 entered the territory where the Piro-speaking Pueblos once had lived. These Indians had not rebelled against Spanish rule. Their towns—Senecú, Socorro, Alamillo, San Pascual, Sevilleta—all were deserted; they had been destroyed by the Apaches. Churches and kivas alike were in ruins. Fray Francisco carefully collected and burned the mutilated sacred images and holy vessels he found.

The first inhabited pueblo that the Spaniards reached was Isleta, in the Tiguex group. Here, too, the Indians had not taken part in the revolt, although after the Spanish withdrawal they had quickly reverted to their old religion; they had destroyed their church and were using its charred walls as a corral for livestock. When Otermín demanded admission to the pueblo, the people refused, and put up token resistance as the Spaniards tried to force their way in on December 6. But Isleta had no taste for warfare, and quickly surrendered; the leaders of the pueblo humbly came forth, weeping, to pledge allegiance to Otermín and to welcome the return of the friars. They insisted that they would have remained good Christians if they had not been compelled by the rebels in the north to go back to paganism. There was another reason for Isleta's ready submission: the pueblo had had a good harvest, and its storage bins were full of corn. In the north, the quarreling rebels were stricken with famine, and Isleta wanted the Spaniards to protect them against a raid by the hungry Indians upriver.

At a ceremony on December 7, the 1,511 people of Isleta formally renewed their loyalty to Spain and received Otermín's pardon for their lapse from Christianity; the children who had been born since the revolt were brought forth to undergo baptism. According to Fray Francisco, the Indians produced "the idols, feathers, powders, masks, and every other thing pertaining to their idolatry and superstition," and these things were "piled in a heap and burned." Then Otermín sent Indian runners to the northern pueblos, bearing word that he would take no vengeance against them if they would yield peacefully.

No reply came from these pueblos, and a few days later a force of seventy men under Otermín's second-in-command, Juan Dominguez de Mendoza, was dispatched on a reconnaissance mission into the district of the rebels. Otermín, meanwhile, would proceed more slowly upriver through the Tiguex group. Assailed by sleet and snow, Mendoza and his men hurried northward through a doleful wasteland of empty villages. The Indians all along the central section of the valley had fled into the hills at the news that the Spaniards had come back, and no one remained in the pueblos except a few old men and women too feeble to leave.

At each of these deserted villages Mendoza, following instructions given him by Otermín, searched for and burned the desecrated and mutilated Christian holy things that the Indians had kept to be the objects of mockery. Then he wrecked the kivas and destroyed kachina masks and other pagan articles. Lastly, by way of punishing the absent Indians for their rebelliousness, he set fire to whatever food supplies the natives had left behind. Ten pueblos were sacked in this fashion.

Continuing upriver, Mendoza entered the Keres-speaking region and came to the pueblos of San Felipe, Santo Domingo, and Cochiti. Here, too, the Indians had run away, and Mendoza prepared to give the towns the treatment he had meted out to the others. But then, outside Cochiti, a defiant army of Indians from the three Keresan pueblos appeared, and, keeping a safe distance, shouted insults at the Spaniards, calling them "horned, bleating he-goats" and worse things. Gradually the fury of the Indians spent itself, though, and after a while one of their chiefs came forward to parley. He was Catiti of Santo Domingo, a key figure in the revolt. Confronted by the Spaniards, he broke down, making a sudden show of remorse and tearfully asking forgiveness for his sins. Popé, he said, had "made them all crazy and was like a whirlwind." After receiving a pardon from Mendoza, Catiti promised to bring all the other rebel leaders to him within a day and a half to surrender.

Mendoza took up lodgings in Cochiti and waited for the fulfillment of Catiti's pledge. Indians began to come to him to beg for pardon; but then one of them whispered to the Spaniards that it was all a trick, that Catiti simply was trying to lull them into relaxing their guard. A rebel army was assembling in the north, Mendoza learned; the Indians at Cochiti planned to steal the horses of the Spaniards, so that they would not be able to escape when the rebels arrived and the massacre began.

The warning had the ring of truth. Hastily Mendoza ordered a withdrawal from Cochiti, and headed south just before Christmas to rejoin Otermín. The governor, during the two weeks of Mendoza's absence, had visited the Tiguex pueblos of Alameda, Puaray, and Sandía, and, finding all three deserted, had destroyed them with fire. He was camped near the ruins of Sandía when Mendoza returned on December 23. It was a frosty meeting: Otermín listened in displeasure to the story of what had happened at Cochiti, and severely criticized his lieutenant for having been so gentle with the Indians. Why had Mendoza not beaten them into submission? Why had he failed to punish them for rebellion by burning their villages? Why had he not sent frequent written reports of the proper style to Otermín? Mendoza replied angrily that he and his men would have been slain if they had attempted to fight the Indians, and that he had had no time to think about filing reports.

Thus the expedition of reconquest, which had seemed in its early days to be capable of achieving its goal, dissolved into bickering between its leader and its second-in-command. The retreat from Cochiti had robbed the Spaniards of their momentum, and now they lost what little will they had had to proceed. The winter was a savage one, with heavy snowfalls almost daily; it seemed suicidal to them to try to make war in such weather, on the home territory of their enemies, with their morale flagging and provisions running low. The news that Tupatú of Picuris was on his way downriver at the head of a large rebel force was the final discouragement. Otermín decided to call the campaign off and go back to El Paso.

When the Spaniards reached Isleta in the final days of 1681 they found a new problem on their hands. The people of Isleta had calculated that the rebels were stronger than the Spaniards, and would surely punish them terribly if they did not hurriedly throw off their newly resumed allegiance to Spain. Therefore, all but 385 of them had fled from Isleta and were rushing northward to offer their services to Tupatú's army. So much for the one apparent accomplishment of Otermín's expedition; Isleta's rebirth of loyalty had lasted less than a month.

He could not now leave the pueblo's 385 Christian Indians to their fate; the rebels probably would slaughter them. So when the Spaniards set out again down the valley on January 2, 1682, these 385 went with them. To keep the pueblo from falling to the rebels, Otermín burned it, along with all the grain and other valuables that could not be carried on the march. The refugees from Isleta were resettled, with Spanish help, at three newly founded pueblos near El Paso, which were named Senecú, Socorro, and Isleta del Sur ("Isleta of the South") after the old pueblos that had been abandoned.

By the middle of February the expedition was back at its starting point, having ended in complete failure. The futile journey left Otermín bitter and despondent, and his report to the viceroy was a gloomy one. He admitted that he could no longer maintain much control over his demoralized, defeated subjects. A mood of despair had infected everyone, and the universal atmosphere of frustration among the Spaniards was leading them into wholesale lawlessness. For example, while marching through New Mexico the expedition had stopped at many of the ruined haciendas and had retrieved valuable goods left behind by the owners. These possessions were supposed to be turned over to the governor to be divided for equal benefit—assuming their original owners were dead—but, Otermín said, the men, acting "with audacious impudence and effrontery," were regarding this loot as their private property, "an offense so general that at present there is no remedy for it." Reconquest of New Mexico with anything less than a major army would be impossible, Otermín asserted. It was hard to gain the cooperation of the present colonists, he said, because they "are accustomed to live very much as they please in everything and at long distances from one another—which was the cause of the loss of New Mexico." And, though his term as governor still had more than a year to run, he asked permission to take a leave of absence for medical reasons, declaring, "My health, sir, what with continuous attacks of headache which I have experienced on this occasion, contracted from the severe cold and extremes of weather in this kingdom, is much impaired and requires some remedy."

From Mexico City, under date of June 25, 1682, came a stern rebuke for Otermín. His request for a leave was denied; he would simply have to suffer through the remainder of his term. He was criticized for poor leadership; the revolt, he was told, would not have come about at all had the Indians not risen up against "the many oppressions which they receive from the Spaniards." No further attempt at reconquest should be made at this time, since the last had been "so unsatisfactory, and the people engaged in it being suspect and discredited." As for the unfortunate Mendoza, he was to stand criminal prosecution for his failure to destroy the northern pueblos.

Thus the unhappy governorship of Don Antonio de Otermín drifted to its close. Of the events at El Paso del Norte between the summer of 1682 and the autumn of 1683 we have little record, other than an account of a brief civil war among the Spanish soldiers, in which an officer was killed. The heroic Fray Francisco de Ayeta concluded his arduous services on behalf of the colonists of New Mexico and went on to new duties elsewhere. To El Paso, finally, came a replacement for Otermín: General Domingo Jironza Petriz de Cruzate, who had distinguished himself leading Spanish troops in battle in Europe. He arrived to take command of the colonists on August 30, 1683, discovering with some dismay that his official residence was to be a dusty hut of twigs and branches.

In New Mexico the ferocious reign of Popé continued. He still held court in the governor's palace at Santa Fe, and still amused himself by mocking the pretensions of the defeated Spaniards. Once, visiting the pueblo of Tanaya, which the Christians had called Santa Ana, Popé staged a scathing parody of a Spanish feast, with himself in the role of governor, sitting at the head of a long table set in Spanish style. Another Indian, at the far end, enacted the part of the father-president. Each of them had a chalice taken from a looted church; Popé rose, bowed, raised his chalice, and with many exaggerated courtly flourishes called forth, "To your paternal reverence's health!" The other Indian responded to the toast with equal formality, lifting his cup and intoning, "Here is to your lordship's health, my lord governor," while roars of laughter echoed in the room.

But there was little cause for laughter otherwise. Popé's government was beginning to collapse. The kachina dances had turned out to be no more helpful in bringing rain than the mass had been; the gods of the Pueblos seemed to have turned against their people. There had not been adequate rainfall for more than twenty years. Apache depredations had forced the abandonment of a score of villages; fighting among the Pueblos themselves had destroyed many more, so that the world of Pueblo life had contracted to nothing more than a few dozen towns lining the river from Taos to a point somewhat above the present-day city of Albuquerque, plus Ácoma and the Hopi and Zuni villages in the west. Even the leaders of the revolt seemed to have incurred the displeasure of the heavens: Catiti, as he entered a kiva for a religious ceremony, suddenly fell down dead while hundreds of horrified Indians looked on.

There was no longer even a pretense at a centralized confederacy of tribes. The Tewas and the Tanos, who had organized the revolt, still were bound to one another in loose alliance, but their Keres-speaking neighbors had pulled free, with each Keresan pueblo governing itself as in the old days. The northern Tiwas of Taos and Picuris were in a more or less constant state of war with the Tewa-Tano alliance, as were the Towas of Pecos and those of the pueblo of Jemez, west of the river. The other Rio Grande tribes had effectively ceased to exist. As we have already seen, the Piro pueblos of southernmost New Mexico had been abandoned even before the revolt, while the pueblos of the southern Tiwas, the Tiguex group, were destroyed by the rebels and the Apache, with Otermín and Mendoza finishing the job in 1681. Many of these people had fled into Hopi country and had founded new villages there.

The aftermath of the revolt had been so disastrous that within a few years the Tanos rebelled against Popé, deposed him, and made the more temperate Tupatú their ruler. But matters did not improve, and shortly the fiery Popé was in command again.

Meanwhile Spain clung to the idea of recapturing New Mexico, although neither the king nor the Mexican viceroy was willing to go to any great trouble to do so. In a royal decree dated September 4, 1683, the king had ordered the reconquest of the lost province "with as little expense as possible to my royal treasury."

Governor Cruzate, who had never set foot in New Mexico, obeyed his command loyally but with no great eagerness. He would reconquer New Mexico if he could; but to him it seemed enough of a challenge simply to hold possession of so impoverished and poorly defended a place as El Paso. The Indians of northern Mexico now were growing uneasy about the presence of the Spaniards in their land, and there had already been a few skirmishes; El Paso itself might very well come under attack before long.

Cruzate persuaded the settlers at El Paso, who had scattered over a wide area, to move closer to the Guadalupe mission at the center of the town. For governmental purposes he erected a sturdy brick building, with an audience hall, a munitions vault, and several other rooms. He applied to Mexico for more soldiers and arms, and did what he could to strengthen the town's defenses. Occasionally he sent military parties out to quell trouble among the Indians of the vicinity. There was constant half-hearted talk of a new invasion of New Mexico.

However, Cruzate's attention was distracted by reports brought to him by Indians concerning "the great kingdom of the Texas," a supposed land of great wealth to the east. Late in 1683 the father-president of the settlement, Fray Nicolás López, boldly entered this unknown country and found the Indians willing to accept Christianity. So enthusiastic were his reports that on December 15 Cruzate dispatched twenty-six men under Juan Dominguez de Mendoza to explore "the Texas." On June 13, 1684, Mendoza officially took possession of this immense new land on behalf of the governor of New Mexico, and hurried back to El Paso to tell Cruzate what he had seen.

It was, he said, "the richest land in all New Spain, for it abounds in grapes, nuts, acorns, berries, plums, buffaloes, rivers with pearls, and mountains full of minerals." While he had been off discovering these things, El Paso had narrowly managed to beat down an uprising of the local Indians; yet, despite the precarious situation of the colony's one town,

Cruzate was so excited by the prospects of Texas that he shortly was asking the viceroy's permission to settle this new domain.

The viceroy acted with unusual swiftness to grant Cruzate's request, for he had heard that the French had entered Texas from the eastern side, and it would be deplorable to let another nation seize such obviously valuable land. Over the next few years, then, most of Cruzate's energy was devoted to heading off the French by extending Spanish authority into Texas; he also led a number of punitive raids against the Indians around El Paso, but did nothing to regain New Mexico.

Cruzate's military exploits in northern Mexico and his entry into Texas brought him into conflict with the governor of New Biscay, who felt that Cruzate was overstepping his authority. New Mexico, after all, was more a state of mind than a Spanish province at the moment, and the governor of New Biscay felt that Cruzate's people should remain close to El Paso until they were ready to go back to their own land. This squabble led in 1686 to Cruzate's removal as governor, probably for political reasons. He was succeeded by Don Pedro Reneros, who took more seriously the king's command to reconquer the lost province.

In 1687 Reneros led the first large-scale Spanish invasion of New Mexico since Otermín's entry of six years before. He went quickly up the now deserted southern stretch of the Rio Grande Valley, and finally came to an inhabited pueblo on October 8. This was Tanaya, or Santa Ana, one of the smaller Keresan villages. The Indians were unfriendly, and Reneros attacked the pueblo, capturing it and setting fire to it. Many Indians were killed and some were captured. The Spaniards then pushed on to the nearby pueblo of Zia, a short distance to the west, where again the Indians greeted the invaders with defiance. Once more Reneros attacked, but this time the natives held firm and drove the Spaniards back. With the defeat at Zia the desire for further combat seemed to go out of Reneros and his men, and they returned immediately to El Paso.

The year 1688 was marked by the death of Popé. The fierce old medicine man had led his people into a freedom they were no longer equipped to handle, and had abused his own position after the revolt; yet he must be considered a potent figure in the history of the American Indian, one of the very few who actually succeeded in halting, if only for a while, the territorial advance of the European conquerors. He was succeeded at the head of the Tewa-Tano alliance once against by Tupatú, a far more stable personality. There was also a change of command among the exiled Spaniards at El Paso, for Reneros had shown himself to be an incompetent governor, and Cruzate was given the office a second time. By now the Mexican viceroy had placed the Texas project in other hands, so Cruzate devoted his full attention to picking up the reconquest of New Mexico where Reneros had dropped it.

With a small army he invaded the Keresan territory in the summer of 1688 and laid siege to Zia. The Indians defended their pueblo vigorously, but suffered heavy losses, and on August 29 the Spaniards took the village after having slain six hundred of its warriors. Four medicine men were caught and executed in the pueblo's plaza, and many of the other people of Zia perished when Cruzate set fire to the town. Some seventy prisoners were taken. Among them was a warrior known to the Spaniards as Bartolomé de Ojeda, who had fought with particular bravery in Zia's defense. Ojeda, before the revolt, had been regarded as *muy Ladino* by the Spaniards—"very Latin." He spoke Spanish well, knew how to read and write, and was a devout Christian. Severely wounded in the battle, he feared he was going to die and surrendered himself, asking that one of Cruzate's friars hear his confession. After this act of renewed faith Ojeda recovered and pledged his loyalty to the Spaniards.

The battle of Zia was the only encounter in Cruzate's New Mexican campaign. He had avenged the defeat of Reneros of the year before, but he realized that he lacked the power to draw any real advantage from his lone victory, and prudently retreated to El Paso with his seventy captives. The expedition had bolstered the pride of the Spaniards, perhaps, but it was basically a futile and wasteful enterprise. Most of the prisoners were sentenced to ten years of slavery by Cruzate as punishment for their departure from Christianity. Bartolomé de Ojeda was released and returned to his people, who were camping a few miles from the ruins of their pueblo; later he served as Zia's governor.

Cruzate planned a more ambitious invasion of New Mexico for 1689, but the project had to be called off when the Indians around El Paso once more went on the warpath. Local disturbances apparently kept Cruzate busy there through that year and most of 1690. Meanwhile a certain Captain Toribio de la Huerta had presented himself to King Charles II in Spain and had volunteered to bring the unruly natives of New Mexico under Spanish rule again, at his own expense, in return for the governorship of the province and the title of marquis. Huerta advertised himself to the king as "one of the first conquerors of the realm of New Mexico . . . and the discoverer of Great Quivira, which is composed of four kings and an emperor." This was obviously nonsense, for if anyone could be said to have discovered Quivira it was Coronado, 150 years earlier, and the first conqueror of New Mexico was Oñate, decades before Huerta was born.

Huerta also claimed to have served Spain for forty years in New Mexico, and to have founded more than thirty towns and mining camps, as well as many churches and convents. This, too, should have seemed implausible to the king's advisers.

One section of Huerta's petition, though, excited the royal court and awoke his Majesty's long-slumbering interest in New Mexico. The captain declared that he "had discovered a place called Sierra Azul more than two hundred leagues long and full of silver," and he had found another place where quicksilver—mercury—could readily be mined. If the king agreed, Huerta would enter New Mexico at once, taking with him five hundred soldiers, and would subdue the Indians so that these mines could be worked for the great profit of everyone.

Up till this point the reconquest of New Mexico had been, in the king's eyes, a mere matter of saving Indian souls and adding some reasonably fertile land to the empire—both desirable goals, but nothing worth making much of an effort to achieve. The promise of rich mines, though, altered everything. Did anyone at the court care that Espejo and Oñate had talked of such mines in the previous century, without producing any wealth? No. Did anyone object that the elderly Huerta seemed unreliable and given to unwarranted boasting? No. On September 13, 1689, the king formally accepted Huerta's proposals and notified his viceroy in Mexico, the Count of Galve, to render all possible aid to Huerta as he made ready for his war of reconquest.

The Count of Galve knew nothing of Huerta, and had someone else in mind for the task of regaining New Mexico. The viceroy's candidate was Don Diego José de Vargas Zapata Luján Ponce de León y Contreras, usually known simply as Don Diego de Vargas. As his lengthy full name implies, Vargas was a man of high ancestry, with ties of blood to several of Spain's greatest families. Early in 1690, before the king's decree concerning Huerta had reached him, the viceroy had invited Vargas to replace Cruzate as governor at El Paso, for Cruzate's term was up and he had expressed a wish to be transferred to a less arduous post. Vargas accepted; and on September 25, 1690, he was sworn in at Mexico City, the viceroy having decided quietly to disregard the king's agreement with Huerta. Vargas was undertaking a triple assignment: to subdue the troublesome tribes around El Paso, to regain New Mexico for Spain, and to find the mines of which Huerta had spoken. If anyone could accomplish these difficult tasks, the viceroy believed, it was Diego de Vargas.

Nor was the viceroy's confidence misplaced. In Vargas he had found a truly extraordinary man, whose courage and gifts of leadership were destined to bring to an end the Pueblo Indians' gallant, unhappy experiment in self-government.

9

The Last Conquistador

At the time he became governor of New Mexico, Don Diego de Vargas was not quite fifty years old. He was an example of the finest type of Spanish grandee: cultured, devout, self-disciplined, elegant, fearing nothing but God. A tall, slender man of aristocratic bearing, Vargas wore black shoulder-length hair, a carefully trimmed mustache, and a slender, pointed beard. He dressed magnificently, affecting the high style of the Spanish court: Dutch linen shirts, white silk hose, ruffled vests embroidered with gold lace, velvet outergarments trimmed with ermine. His expression was solemn and his gaze was steady; he had the cool, self-assured look of a born commander of men.

His family was a wealthy and distinguished one, with a record of accomplishment and national service going back to the eleventh century. Included in his pedigree were generals, governors, scholars, a bishop, and an ambassador. St. Isidore the Laborer, the beloved patron saint of Madrid, had been a farmhand on the estate of a twelfth-century Vargas. The sixteenth-century mystic nun St. Teresa of Avila belonged to one branch of the family. The Vargases occupied a great palace in Madrid and mansions nearly as imposing in Granada and Mexico City; they owned valuable land in many other parts of Spain and the overseas empire, drawing revenue from olive orchards, vineyards, salt deposits, pastures, and farms.

It was taken for granted that anyone born into such splendid advantages should devote himself to the welfare of the kingdom rather than spending his days in idle consumption of luxuries. As a young man Diego de Vargas served as a military officer, and took part in Spain's European wars, fighting on several Italian battlefields. In 1672 he came to Mexico, where at first he served in minor administrative posts, as the mayor of this town or the chief justice of that one; but his efficiency and skill won him a series of rapid promotions, and within a few years he had become one of the overseers of the kingdom's mineral supply, with special charge over the mining of mercury. He served so well in this post that the king, in a decree of 1683, brought him to the attention of the current Mexican viceroy, the Count of Paredes, suggesting that Vargas be given positions of high responsibility within the Mexican government. From that time on Vargas remained close to the seat of power in Mexico, retaining his authority and influence when the Count of Galve replaced the Count of Paredes as viceroy.

To the Count of Galve, Vargas seemed precisely the man to resolve the dreary and unpleasant New Mexican situation. For a full decade, now, the Spaniards in Mexico had been forced to tolerate the existence of an independent Indian territory on their northern frontier, in what had formerly been a province of the empire of Spain; the time had come to end that absurd embarrassment.

On February 22, 1691, Vargas arrived in El Paso to replace Governor Cruzate. The splendors of Madrid and the grandeur of Mexico City now lay a world away; El Paso, the capital-in-exile of the provinces he supposedly governed, was a shabby, dusty village, inhabited by settlers whose eyes were dull with the memory of shameful defeat. Yet the El Paso garrison made at least a pretense of a brave show for their impressive-looking new commander: clad in their leather armor, the troops paraded smartly in the town square to welcome him.

Almost at once, a current of new life ran through the village. There seemed hope of actually reconquering the north, as there never had been under Otermín, Reneros, or Cruzate. The prospect of finding Huerta's mines, of attaining the mineral bonanza that had never been theirs in the days before the revolt, inspired the colonists with sudden eagerness to cross the Rio Grande. A letter from the viceroy to Vargas, dated May 27, 1691, made the quicksilver mines an explicit part of the governor's responsibilities. "From the accounts of people who have lived in the region up north," the viceroy wrote, "I understand that within the rebellious area of New Mexico lies a province called Moqui [the Hopi country], and that twelve leagues from it in the direction of the Rio Grande is situated one of the most important of its ranges from which were extracted the minerals or vermilion-colored soil used by the Indians to daub themselves; it was formerly used by all kinds of people. . . ." This substance was as soft as butter, and left purple stains on the hands; it was said to be a high-quality ore of mercury. The Count of Galve requested Vargas to investigate the place where it was found and make a full report to him.

Vargas questioned three friars and eight soldiers familiar with the western part of New Mexico, and they confirmed that such a quicksilver mine did exist. It was somewhere near the Hopi pueblo of Oraibi, they thought. On August 26,

1691, Vargas sent transcripts of their statements to Mexico City and requested the making of jars of a special design, for the transportation of ore samples. "I will risk myself and go with the men that your excellency will designate," he declared, "and may your excellency believe that I shall do everything in my power to discover this mine, make investigations among the Indians by treating them kindly, and do everything possible." If the natives proved hostile, he would "try first to win them over by gentleness alone, but, if some should prove recalcitrant, they would be wiped out at once."

Before he could begin his expedition into New Mexico, though, Vargas felt he had to secure the region around El Paso. The Indians of northern Mexico and western Texas still were causing problems, despite Cruzate's almost constant campaigns to pacify these turbulent desert-dwellers; Vargas did not wish to go north while there was a possibility that his line of withdrawal to El Paso might be cut by Indian trouble to his rear. Therefore he spent the latter half of 1691 and the first part of 1692 subduing the natives of the border region, and only when, after a series of vigorous sorties, he had suppressed all disturbances close to El Paso, did he start organizing his northward march.

In Mexico City, meanwhile, the viceroy was mobilizing the resources of his government on Vargas' behalf. He consulted first with Otermín and Cruzate, asking these former governors what they knew about the alleged quicksilver mines. Cruzate replied that he had heard stories of such mines, and even had tested some ore that supposedly came from them, but the results had not been good; he suggested that Vargas concentrate on reconquering the province, and leave investigation of the mines for some other time. But Otermín felt certain that the mines did exist, and believed Vargas should go directly to the Hopi country to search for them, taking up the problem of the reconquest of the Rio Grande region afterward. Since the opinions of these two authorities were contradictory, the viceroy referred the matter to his council of advisers. They voted in favor of providing Vargas with soldiers, and recommended that he bring the rebellious province under Spanish control before looking for mines.

This decision was communicated to Vargas in the spring of 1692. He immediately invited the settlers in El Paso and the surrounding regions of northern Mexico to volunteer for the New Mexico expedition, promising to pay—out of his own funds—all their living expenses not only during the campaign but in the months before the expedition set out for the north. He also asked the viceroy to arrange for the governor of New Biscay to provide fifty additional soldiers. The campaign would begin, Vargas thought, early that summer. He set July 12 as the date of departure.

One minor matter remained unsettled: the question of Don Toribio de la Huerta, who had been chosen by the king to lead the invasion that Vargas was about to launch. At a meeting in Mexico City on May 28, 1692, the viceroy and his councillors officially decided to ignore the king's wishes. They set forth their reasons in a lengthy document, which noted that "the governor [Vargas] is a man of outstanding qualities, blood, and responsibility, and he has many advantages over Don Toribio de la Huerta who (according to our information) would not perform his duty so faithfully. . . ." Thus they ruled that Vargas was "far more eligible for this highly important mission."

At El Paso, Vargas assembled his men and waited for the fifty reinforcements from New Biscay to arrive. They did not arrive; the governor of New Biscay had written to the viceroy, expressing his doubt that New Mexico could be conquered, and arguing that the high cost of maintaining settlements there made it undesirable even to attempt a reconquest. This dispute, unknown to Vargas, went on through May and June. His starting date of July 12 came, and still the New Biscayans failed to appear. On July 13 Vargas wrote to the viceroy to say that he was ready to go, but had not received the expected reinforcements. His impatience mounted. Now it was the beginning of August, and he was still at El Paso. He estimated that he would need four or five months to carry out the reconquest; this delay meant his army would still be in New Mexico when winter began, something he had hoped to avoid. On August 16, still expecting the fifty New Biscayans momentarily, Vargas gave orders for part of his force to start crossing the Rio Grande. This advance party, under the command of Captain Roque de Madrid, consisted of about half of Vargas' troops, along with wagons, livestock, and pack animals. The anticipated reinforcements still did not materialize, and by August 21 Vargas could wait no longer. He left word at El Paso for the men from New Biscay to join him in the north as quickly as possible, and impulsively set out with the rest of his army to catch up to Roque de Madrid. He overtook the advance party on August 24.

Thus the brave army of reconquest went forth, marching under the same banner of heavy yellow silk that Oñate had carried joyously up the river in 1598 and that Otermín had brought down river in despair in 1680. Vargas' forces amounted to less than two hundred men. Of these, sixty were Spanish soldiers from El Paso, men who had once lived in New Mexico, and a hundred were Tiwa-speaking Pueblo warriors, recruited from the new villages of Socorro, Senecú, and Isleta del Sur that the refugees from Isleta had founded in 1682. The rest were servants, grooms, and friars. There was also one Indian of the north in the expedition: Bartolomé de Ojeda of Zia, who had fought so valiantly against the Spaniards in 1687 and 1688. Ojeda had agreed to serve as Vargas' interpreter and chief scout.

Vargas did not expect to bring all of New Mexico under control on this expedition. He hoped merely to discover the true state of affairs in the province, and to regain the allegiance of such pueblos as were willing to submit peacefully. Then, in 1693, he planned to return with a much larger army and subdue by force any villages that continued to resist Spanish authority.

According to Ojeda, the political situation in the land of the Pueblos was chaotic. The Keresan pueblos of the Rio Grande were at war with the Tewas and Tanos; the Towas of Pecos and the Tiwas of Taos feared the Tiwas of Picuris; the Hopi and Zuni villages were at odds with the Keresans of Ácoma; and the Apache were causing general confusion everywhere. No pueblo trusted any other pueblo, and such alliances as were formed were constantly on the verge of dissolving in the widespread anarchy. This was a condition Vargas hoped to exploit.

The first two weeks of the northern march were uneventful. It was late summer, heat hung close on the land, and the army moved slowly through the baking countryside without seeing a living soul. The southern group of pueblos—the old Socorro, Senecú, Isleta, and the rest up to Sandía—had all been destroyed years before, and no attempt had been made to rebuild them. On September 9 Vargas made camp at the abandoned hacienda of a settler named Mexia, some sixty-six miles south of Santa Fe, in the vicinity of the present-day city of Albuquerque. Here he chose to establish his main base. Quickly the men fortified the ruined ranchhouse with a wooden stockade; smoke signals, perhaps those of Apache, could be seen in the hills, although no enemies appeared.

Vargas left most of the wagons and supplies here, with four-teen Spaniards and fifty of the Indian allies to guard the base, under the command of Captain Rafael Téllez. The next day he continued northward, taking with him about forty Spanish soldiers and the other fifty Indians.

After twelve hours of hard marching on a road so poor that he was twice forced to detour across the Rio Grande, Vargas came to the Keresan pueblo of Cochiti at three in the morning on September 11. He approached the town cautiously, for his Indian scouts had warned him that Cochiti was prepared to offer vigorous resistance. But the pueblo turned out to be empty, though there were signs of very recent occupation. Vargas concluded that its people, warned of the Spaniards' approach, had slipped off to the pueblo of Santo Domingo, about eight miles downstream on the other side of the river. After pausing to mount fresh horses, the troops rode off toward that village.

Shortly after sunrise they reached Santo Domingo, only to find the place in ruins. Vargas later learned that the in-habitants of this and several other towns had withdrawn to the mountains after Cruzate's destruction of Zia in 1688, and had not yet found courage to return.

There was nothing now to do except go on to Santa Fe, some 30 miles away. They set out on the afternoon of the 11th; but the road had almost vanished from lack of use, and when they camped that night they had covered only six miles. The next day they began to ascend a trail leading up a steep mesa overlooking the Santa Fe region, and in the afternoon, after going nine miles, Vargas called a halt to rest at the abandoned Tano pueblo of Tziguma, while scouts went out to survey the territory ahead. The scouts returned with word that they had seen fresh hoofprints, but no Indians, and about sunset the Spaniards resumed their advance, continuing through the chilly night until darkness forced another halt at eleven o'clock. After exploring the woods, Vargas decided to go forward again about two that morning, and shortly they could see Santa Fe.

At this point the father-president, Fray Francisco Corvera, held a brief religious service, and Vargas gave careful instructions to his men. No one was to fire a gun or make any other warlike gesture unless Vargas first drew his sword. When they came to the open fields by the walls of the city, Vargas would give another signal, at which the soldiers were to rush forward, crying out the words of the *Gloria:* "Glory be to the blessed sacrament of the altar!"

About four in the morning on September 13, Vargas and his men crept up to the city that once had been the capital of Spanish New Mexico. The Indians had occupied Santa Fe for a dozen years; most of those who lived there now were Tanos from the Galisteo region, who had been driven from their pueblos by Apache raids soon after the revolt. The city had taken on a strange hybrid look, for many ruined Spanish buildings still stood, displaying the terrible scars of the seige of 1680, but between the charred, roofless hulks the Indians had constructed large, many-roomed houses in their own style, so that a kind of pueblo sprawled across the Santa Fe of the past. A kiva had been built in the middle of the plaza; the palace of the governors was now an Indian fort. Everything seemed shabby and dilapidated, as if Santa Fe were a tangible symbol of the way the Pueblo revolt had turned sour so soon after victory had been achieved.

All was still. In this high country a cold night wind blew, though it was only late summer. The Indians slept. Vargas gave the signal for the *Gloria,* and his men ran toward the walls, shouting out again and again, "Glory be to the blessed sacrament of the altar!"

Amazed Indians appeared on the roof of the palace of the governors. "Who is there?" they called. "Who are you?"

Vargas ordered the *Gloria* proclaimed once more. One of his Indian interpreters then cried in the Tano tongue that the Spaniards had come back to rule the land again, and were willing to forgive the people for their great sins. But dawn had not yet come, and the Spaniards could not be seen clearly; the Indians of Santa Fe insisted that it was all a lie, that this must be some war party from Pecos, or perhaps a band of Apache. Again the soldiers shouted the *Gloria*. The Indians listened to the Spanish words, and after a pause said, "If you are Spaniards, why do you not fire guns? Fire a gun, and we will be sure."

To this the firm voice of Governor Vargas responded, "Be calm. I am a Catholic, and when the sun rises you will see the Blessed Virgin on my flag."

Even this did not convince those in the city. They asked Vargas to let them hear a Spanish war trumpet. Vargas gestured; a trumpeter put his instrument to his lips, and a drummer played a long military roll. At these familiar sounds the skepticism of the Indians vanished, and suddenly, under the impact of the discovery that the Spaniards really were at their walls, they flew into a panicky rage. Shouting, leaping about, screaming abuse, they howled at the Spaniards for nearly an hour. Vargas quietly ordered his men into strategic positions at the entrances to the city, and sent a squad to cut the ditch through which the water supply ran. Seeing this, the Indians began to gather stones and other weapons, and to pile up huge beams and boulders to block the Spaniards from entering.

The sun now had risen. Vargas spoke again, inviting the Indians to surrender, and promising a full pardon. Take off your helmet, the Indians called; let us see your face. And serenely Vargas removed his helmet, riding forward until he stood, bareheaded and vulnerable, directly below a line of Indians who stood with drawn bows. The secret of those old *conquistadores* Cortés and Pizarro had been just such supreme self-confidence, just such unshakeable faith in divine protection; and Vargas, almost two centuries later, the last of the *conquistadores,* used the same tactics to awe the Indians. Again he offered a pardon. He showed a cross and a rosary; he pointed to three friars, and said they would absolve the Indians of past sins. From above, an Indian known as Bolsa, "the Pouches," because of his big cheeks, asked why the Indians should surrender. They would only be forced to rebuild the Spanish houses and churches, would they not? And if they refused, or if they did not work hard enough, they would be whipped, as they were whipped before the revolt, would they not? Bolsa mentioned the names of three Spanish officers who had been feared for their cruelty in the old days, and Vargas assured him that none of these men, nor any who might behave in their fashion, had come to New Mexico this time.

He gave the Indians an hour to think over his words, and went back to his troops. A breakfast of biscuits and hot chocolate was served; then the Spaniards moved their supply carts close to the walls and brought their two bronze cannons into position for attack. While these preparations for siege were being made, an armed Indian came out of the city, walking with a defiant swaggering stride. Vargas offered the man his hand, but the Indian refused it. What did he want? He asked that two friars come into Santa Fe with him. At this, several of the Franciscans made ready to go, but Vargas told them, with a gesture, to wait. His sentries at the far side of the city were giving an alarm.

Bands of Indians, some on horseback and some on foot,

were descending from a nearby ridge. They all were armed, and apparently had come from the surrounding pueblos to aid the people of Santa Fe. Calmly Vargas sent squads of his soldiers to hold these native reinforcements in check; his troops were now divided into so many small groups that only a dozen men remained with him. But the newcomers did not give battle: the strange confidence displayed by the Spaniards intimidated them.

We have two sources for the events of this day. One is Vargas' own letter to the viceroy, written the following month; the other is a pamphlet called *Mercurio Volante* ("the Flying Mercury"), a newspaperlike account of Vargas' expedition published in Mexico City in 1693 by the historian Don Carlos de Siguenza y Góngora. The *Mercurio* tells us that among the Indians who had just arrived was the chief of one of the Keresan pueblos:

> When this individual was brought into the presence of the general [Vargas], his good will was so completely won by kind treatment and words that he went into the city and assured his people energetically "that the Spaniards were not trying to punish them, but rather to restore them to the fold of the Catholic Church from which their apostasy had separated them, and to the allegiance of the Crown of Spain which, through their revolt, they had renounced." The only reply of the Indians was "that they would all die before they would do any such thing, and since he, forgetting his duty to his native land, had become friendly to its enemies, the Spaniards, he could go away and die with them." He returned greatly displeased by this answer.

In an unhurried way the Spaniards went on readying an attack—loading their cannons, piling gunpowder against the city walls to blow them open, cleaning their guns. They did all this in the open, presenting easy targets for the Indian archers on the walls. But the soldiers "showed no concern for the risk and danger of their lives," Vargas wrote, and, the *Mercurio* tells us, "God suddenly softened the obstinate spirit of the Indians. Filled with dread by the firm courage that they had observed in our men, they proposed that 'if the artillery and armed men were first removed, they would come out and parley with the general, who should be unarmed.'" Vargas replied that he had made no threats, and therefore saw no need to withdraw his soldiers; the Indians should have faith in his good intentions and come out although the troops were right there.

Most of the afternoon was consumed by these diplomatic maneuvers. Finally an Indian emerged from the city, unarmed; Vargas descended from his horse and met him with such warmth and friendliness that it astonished the watching natives. The governor and the Indian held a long, amiable conversation. Then, timidly, two more Indians came forth. Vargas embraced them also. Now a pair of friars went into the city to offer blessings, and suddenly all tensions evaporated; scores of natives flocked around Vargas, asking to make peace, praying to be forgiven.

Vargas offered peace to them, he wrote, "with great love, as I stood there dismounted, embracing them, shaking hands with them, and speaking to them with tender and loving words. . . . I told them to make this known to the rest, who had not come down. . . ." It was now six in the evening. Though Vargas could have entered Santa Fe at this point, he chose not to do so; it was another shrewd stroke in the campaign of psychological warfare that he was waging, for it would allow those Indians whom he had befriended to win over the many within the city who still were hostile. Leaving only a few men on guard outside Santa Fe, Vargas gave orders that the rest of his men, with all supplies and the cannons, should withdraw to a point at a considerable distance. Before he parted from the Indians he told them that when he returned the next day he expected to find each of them with a cross about his neck, and a large cross standing in the patio of the palace of the governors.

Lifting the siege this way was a bold, risky step. But, Vargas declared, "I decided to place some trust in fate." As night fell, he led his troops away from Santa Fe, and they spent a watchful night in their camp, wondering if their gamble would be successful.

In the morning—it was September 14, 1692—Vargas went back to Santa Fe. He wore not his gleaming armor but rather an elegant suit of court dress, although he was armed. When the Spaniards came to the city they were met outside by a large number of Indian leaders, who greeted them peacefully and invited Vargas to enter, and celebrate the mass in the palace. However, the *Mercurio Volante* declares, "the Indians insisted stubbornly and obstinately, though at the same time submissively and obsequiously, that only the general, the reverend father-president, and six soldiers without their arquebuses, should come in so that the people would not get excited. 'He who takes no risks to win an immortal name,' said the intrepid general in reply to this, 'accomplishes nothing;' and so, piously invoking the aid of the Most Holy Mary, he marched in."

Vargas' officers had opposed the idea of his placing himself so trustingly at the mercy of the Indians, and they watched uneasily as the governor, the father-president, and six soldiers filed through the narrow gate. Their dismay increased when the gate slammed shut behind the Spanish delegation the instant the eight men had gone in. Within, Vargas found armed Indians on every rooftop, and crisply told them to come down, leaving their weapons inside their houses. They obeyed him. Then, says the *Mercurio,* "unperturbed and even with great dignity and composure he went on to the central square. There the Indians had just set up a beautiful cross." Waiting for the Indians to grow quiet, he addressed them in Spanish, telling them that "our monarch and lord, King Charles II," was graciously willing to forgive them for their renunciation of the Christian faith, for the murder of friars and the desecration of churches, for the slaughter of settlers, and for the destruction of Spanish towns and haciendas, provided they would "penitently and tearfully" return to their Christian beliefs and swear allegiance to the king.

The Indians agreed to both requests, whereupon Vargas announced loudly that he now repossessed "the city of Santa Fe, capital of the realm of New Mexico, together with its provinces and all its pueblos, in the name of the Catholic Majesty of the king, our lord, Charles II." He strode through the throngs of natives, holding the royal banner raised in one hand, while the Indians shouted, "Long live the king!" Then everyone knelt before the cross while the father-president sang the hymn of praise to God, *Te Deum Laudamus.*

Now the gate was thrown wide, and remained open thereafter. The father-president celebrated the mass in the city plaza; then the friars began the task of baptizing all those who had been born since the time of the uprising. There would be 969 such baptisms in the next few days.

Delegations of Indians came to Vargas in Santa Fe to declare their loyalty. One striking confirmation of the degree of disunity among the Pueblos was provided by messengers from the Keresan pueblo of San Felipe, who pledged allegiance to Vargas and spoke of their desire to help him in bringing "death to the Tewas." The governors of two Tano pueblos—San Lázaro and San Cristóbal—arrived and submitted to Vargas, as did those of the Tewa pueblos of San Juan and Tesuque. Vargas also learned that Tupatú, the most powerful of the surviving rebel chieftains, had come to the nearby pueblo of San Juan, but hesitated to continue on to Santa Fe.

Tupatú was the governor of the Tiwa pueblo of Picuris, but, since the death of Popé, he had come to exercise authority over many of the Tano and Tewa pueblos besides. Gaining his support was vital to Vargas' program, and the governor immediately sent one of his own rosaries to Tupatú as a guarantee of safe conduct. Tupatú replied that he would come at once, and on September 16 he appeared outside Santa Fe, leading three hundred armed Indians. The *Mercurio Volante* says that Tupatú "was mounted on a beautiful horse and carried a musket with a pouch of powder and lead; on his forehead was a mother-of-pearl shell like a crown, and he was dressed in Spanish style, though he wore deerskin. Sixty paces from the general's tent he made a halt and his guard of Indians formed themselves into a squadron. After dismounting, he came toward the tent with great dignity and, with three sweeping bows, he knelt before Don Diego, who was standing outside, and kissed his hand." Vargas embraced the Indian, and they exchanged gifts, Tupatú offering robes of bison skin, Vargas presenting a fine horse. They drank chocolate together, and Vargas addressed Tupatú by his long-renounced Christian baptismal name, Luis. He offered his allegiance to Spain and was forgiven for his role in the rebellion.

The next day Tupatú and his brother Lorenzo paid another call on Vargas. Luis Tupatú remarked that during the time when he had ruled the Pueblos, certain tribes—particularly the Towas of Pecos and Jemez, the Tiwas of Taos, and some of the Keresan people—had refused to acknowledge his supremacy. He asked whether Vargas, as a sign of their new friendship, would help him make war against Pecos and Taos, the villages which had most vehemently scorned him.

Vargas replied that he was in fact planning to march against Pecos in a few days, and would be glad to accept Tupatú's aid if it became necessary to attack that or any other village. But he made it clear that he would not punish any pueblo merely because its people were enemies of Tupatú, but rather only because they persisted in rebellion against Spain. Even on these terms, Tupatú agreed to join forces with the Spaniards. It did not matter to him what the pretext for battle was, so long as Vargas helped him defeat those who had defied him.

On September 21, after waiting a few days in the futile hope that the fifty soldiers from New Biscay would finally show up, Vargas set forth at dawn for Pecos. He was accompanied by most of the Spanish and Indian soldiers with whom he had begun the expedition, and by Tupatú's three hundred warriors. Their route took them through the empty Galisteo region, where they made camp the first night. As they were about to begin the second day's march, they heard two signal shots, and then seven unfamiliar Spaniards rode up. They were men of New Biscay: the reinforcements had arrived after all, more than two months late, and the other forty-three soldiers were now on their way from Santa Fe to join Vargas' army.

Shortly they arrived, and what was now quite an imposing force moved on toward Pecos, which they reached at daybreak on September 23. This was one of the largest of the pueblos, with lofty buildings of red clay, four and five stories high, five plazas, and sixteen kivas. It held about two thousand people but its inhabitants had taken refuge in the mountains when they learned that Vargas was coming toward them. He sent scouts into the hills who captured twenty or thirty Indians, as well as a young Spaniard, the son of the hacienda-owner Cristóbal de Anaya, who had been held captive since 1680, when the Indians had murdered his father and the rest of his family. After twelve years the boy could barely speak Spanish. Vargas turned him over to his only surviving relative, his uncle, Francisco de Godoy, who was one of Vargas' artillery officers.

Treating the Indian prisoners with his customary kindness, Vargas gave one a rosary and told him to go to the hiding place of his people and urge them to come out. But neither this messenger nor three others sent after him returned; the Pecos folk were too frightened to show themselves. After a few days Vargas released the remaining captives and returned to Santa Fe.

On September 29 he departed once again for a tour of the northern pueblos, with Luis Tupatú riding at his side. They reached Tesuque that afternoon; the next day they visited three other Tewa villages; on October 1 they entered two more. October 2 saw them in Santa Clara and San Juan, October 3 at San Lázaro and San Cristóbal, October 5 at Picuris. Without exception these pueblos welcomed the arrival of the Spaniards; apparently they had had enough of independence, after a dozen years of hunger, sickness, and civil war. The *Mercurio Volante* comments that

in deference to Don Luis Tupatú, who ordered them to do so, an impressive reception was given to the governor, the missionaries, and to the whole expedition in all of these villages. All the inhabitants came forth bearing crosses, and along the roads were exceedingly odd arches of bulrushes and flowers. These apostates were consecrated anew to the church and asked for the baptism of their children with the greatest eagerness. When they were taken back into the possession of the Catholic Majesty of our monarch and lord, Charles II, all this was celebrated with general rejoicing and festive dances.

A snowstorm began while Vargas was at Picuris, lasting into the following day. Nevertheless he insisted on continuing on to Taos, and reached it at four in the morning on October 7, only to find the big pueblo deserted. Fresh tracks in the snow told the story: fear had led the people to flee in the night. Vargas sent out messengers who followed the tracks, found the Taos people, and gave them assurances of the Spanish governor's good will. Gradually they overcame their caution and returned to their pueblo, where a happy ceremony of reconciliation took place.

But not everything was sweetness and joy. Vargas learned from the Indians of Taos that a conspiracy against him had been organized: the men of Pecos, Jemez, Cochiti, and Santo Domingo planned to ambush him, aided by Hopi and Zuni warriors and even some Apache. Faced with the prospect of serious trouble for the first time, Vargas decided to return quickly to Santa Fe, equip his men with fresh horses and ammunition, and take to the offensive against those villages that were apparently still in rebellion.

From Santa Fe, on October 16, Vargas sent a long letter to the viceroy which described the success he had enjoyed thus far in restoring the Pueblos to their former allegiance. He told of his bloodless victories, of the many baptisms, of the eagerness of the Indians to become Christians again. But he was under no illusions about the permanence of what he had achieved. The only way to hold the province for Spain was to fill it with Spaniards; he urged that five hundred families be sent at once to settle in New Mexico, and that a garrison of a hundred soldiers be stationed at Santa Fe. Anything less, he said, would be "to cast a grain of salt into the sea."

The next day Vargas was on the march again. He headed for Pecos with sixty soldiers, sending another detachment of men with two heavy artillery pieces toward Santo Domingo. Late on the afternoon of October 17 Pecos came into view. Trails of smoke were rising from the openings in the pueblo's roofs, telling Vargas that this time its people had not fled. He paused to prepare a careful plan of attack. When he was still nearly a mile from the village, a band of more than 400 armed Indians appeared; Vargas formed his troops into a wedge, with himself at the point in front, and went steadily forward into them. But the Indians had not come to make war. The tales they had heard of Vargas' just and reasonable nature had impressed the leaders of Pecos, and the fact that he had not laid waste to their town when he found it empty in September counted heavily with them. Vargas' sense of his own moral superiority was perhaps his most powerful weapon, for, sublimely confident of his heaven-granted right to govern these people, he was able in some mysterious word-less way to transmit that feeling to them and lead them to submit. After a brief parley, the Indians invited him to enter their village.

At Pecos on October 18 Vargas' friars performed 248 baptisms, and Vargas reconstituted the colonial governmental structure of the pueblo, swearing into office a number of newly appointed officials. That evening he left, marching through the Tano region and passing the deserted pueblos of Galisteo and San Marcos. Now he entered the Keres-speaking district, sending messengers ahead bearing friendly words and gifts for the Keresan chiefs. Several of these chiefs come forth to meet him, and on October 20 Vargas was admitted peacefully to the supposedly rebellious pueblo of Cochiti, where, as bitter winds whipped gray dust through the plaza, 103 adults and children were baptized not far from the kiva. Representatives from the Keresan pueblo of San Felipe also pledged allegiance to Vargas. It began to appear as though the reports of Indian hostility had been greatly exaggerated.

He headed on to the pueblo of Zia, which he reached on the evening of October 23. The village had never been rebuilt after its sacking by Cruzate in 1688, and no one lived there; the Spaniards made camp for the night in its ruins. One of Vargas' men discovered a large church-bell that the Indians had buried in the days of the revolt. The governor ordered it buried again for safekeeping. In the morning they marched westward, and in the hills twelve miles from Zia the Spaniards found that pueblo's people, living as refugees in a shabby encampment. Once again the magic of Vargas' personality was invoked: he merely had to present himself outside the settlement, and the people of Zia emerged, crosses in their hands, to pay homage to him. With Bartolomé de Ojeda serving as interpreter, Vargas greeted Malacate, the cacique of Zia, and accepted from him the submission of his village. There were 123 baptisms, and Malacate, who was old and ill, invited Vargas to preside over the installation of a new chief, Cristóbal. At the ceremony Cristóbal swore to be loyal to the church and to the Spanish king. Then Vargas ordered the Zia folk to return to their old pueblo, "since the walls are strong and in good condition," and to rebuild their church. When they pointed out that they had no tools, he promised to give them some. A wild, noisy dance of celebration, marking the end of Zia's unhappy years of independence, concluded the visit of the Spaniards.

Nine miles to the northwest lay the Towa-speaking pueblo

of Jemez, where anti-Spanish feelings were exceptionally bitter. Living near Jemez were the Indians who had fled from Santo Domingo after Cruzate's invasion of 1688; they, too, were seething with rage. There were also some Apache of the group known today as Navajo; a kind of alliance had sprung up between them and the people of Jemez, with hatred of the Spaniards the common bond. Malacate of Zia told Vargas that Jemez had invited him to join in an attack on Vargas' party, but that he had refused and had advised them not to carry out the plot.

Whatever uneasiness he felt as he approached this zone of danger, Vargas was careful to seem outwardly tranquil and contemptuous of fear. He found the warriors of Jemez, with their Apache allies and some of the men of Santo Domingo, menacingly arrayed along the crest of a hill near the village, heavily armed. As the Spaniards marched toward them, the Indians began to throw dust into their eyes; but Vargas warned his men to show no sign of anger at this. Whoever made a threatening gesture toward an Indian, he said, would suffer the death penalty. Under this imposed attitude of tolerance the Spaniards went grimly through the clouds of dust, and the Indians, seeing that they had failed to goad their foes into attacking, dropped back, dismayed. Vargas' display of composure led the natives to look upon him as invincible. Therefore they admitted him to their pueblo without resistance, and even tried to pretend that the throwing of dust had merely been a festive greeting. Standing in the plaza of Jemez, he saw tense faces everywhere, and armed Indians outside every house; but, though the threatening undercurrents of massacre were unmistakable, Vargas as usual cowed the Indians into promising allegiance to Christ and the king. The same thing happened at the camp of the displaced Santo Domingans: tension, the possibility of a sudden desperate attack, and ultimately a peaceful, if precarious, yielding.

The Spaniards now doubled back southward to the base they had established at the hacienda of Mexia, near present-day Albuquerque. Here Vargas dismissed the Piro Indian allies who had accompanied him from El Paso; they were exhausted by the long campaign and by the rigors of the cold weather of the north, to which they were unaccustomed, and, since no military problems were developing, he felt he had no further need of them. If necessary, Vargas thought, he could make use of the Tano and Tewa troops that Tupatú had placed at his disposal.

He also released some of the Spaniards who had marched with him, replacing them with eight of the soldiers who had spent the last seven weeks guarding the base at Mexia. Then he began to plan the most challenging task of his campaign: the invasion of the western pueblos, where even at the best of times Spanish rule had been shaky.

Some of Vargas' officers proposed leaving this project for the following year. The men and horses were tired, they said; the winter was coming on; the Indians of the western villages were stubborn and unfriendly. Vargas overruled them, though, declaring that he did not wish to lose the momentum of reconquest he had already established, since plainly this expedition had received the special blessing of heaven. On October 30 he departed from Mexia, with Ácoma the first stop.

To his chagrin, Vargas had discovered at the last moment that Tupatú could not spare very many Indian soldiers for the proposed campaign against the western pueblos, for it was harvest season, and the early snowfalls were imperiling the ungathered crops. Since it would have been unreasonable to pull his Tano and Tewa allies away from their responsibilities at home, Vargas did not press the issue, but neither did he cancel his western invasion. He took with him only eighty-nine Spanish soldiers and just thirty Indian troops, the most that Tupatú could provide.

With this light force he sped westward in crisp, cold weather and came to high Ácoma on November 3. The mesa-top pueblo's inhabitants looked down, brandished their weapons, and told the Spaniards to go away. Vargas, imperturbable, invited them to submit, offering full pardon for past offenses. The Indians refused; then, as Vargas continued to speak gently to them, they began to consider the proposition seriously. But they were too fearful of Spanish vengeance at Ácoma to yield even to the magnetic Vargas; the monstrous punishment inflicted on them a century ago by Oñate was still a fiery memory. So they suggested to Vargas that he go on to Zuni, giving them some time to think things over, and refused to let him ascend the mesa.

Vargas would not accept that. He knew the history of this pueblo—how Juan de Zaldívar had been slaughtered there with most of his men in 1598, how Vicente de Zaldívar had captured it through surprise attack the following year. He waited out the night, and on the morning of November 4 performed one of his most daring exploits: with nine companions he scrambled up the craggy face of the mesa and presented himself in the midst of the natives. His startling accomplishment of the almost impossible climb awed them into submission; friars were allowed to come to the summit, and eighty-seven children were baptized. After the customary ceremony of reconciliation, the Spaniards departed.

A week later they were in the Zuni country. Here Vargas found that Apache attacks had forced the Zuni to abandon their villages and found a new settlement on a high mesa known as Kiákima. As the Spaniards neared the mesa, an

Apache band made a dash at them, and captured some of their cattle before being driven off. But there was no opposition at all from the Zuni, although Vargas had been told that they had sworn to destroy him. Courteously, hospitably, the Indians permitted Vargas to climb their mesa and enter their town. On November 14 came the formal rite of allegiance, and three hundred baptisms were performed.

Among the Zuni the Spaniards found the only evidence they had seen in all of New Mexico that some trace of Christian faith had remained after the revolt of 1680. Vargas was taken to a room in which two candles were burning on an altar; around it were an image of Christ, a portrait of St. John the Baptist, several sacred vessels, and some religious books, including a volume of the works of St. Teresa of Avila, the second cousin of Vargas' grandmother. These things, he was told, had belonged to the friar stationed at the Zuni pueblo of Halona, and for some reason had been carefully preserved after that friar's martyrdom in the revolt. "This discovery," the *Mercurio Volante* declares, "produced a profound feeling of emotion and devotion in the general and also in some of his officers who had come in; embracing the leaders of these Indians and thanking them repeatedly, he assured them that from this time henceforth he would look after them with special affection." Vargas gathered up the holy objects to take them with him to El Paso for reconsecration.

He prepared to go on to the Hopi country. Since about two dozen of his men were too weary for further marching, he left them camped among the Zuni with most of the baggage and supplies, and went forward with a lightly armed force of sixty-three Spaniards and Tupatú's Indians. It was 120 miles to the first Hopi mesa, with only three waterholes along the way, and blizzards imposed great hardships on the men. Thirsty, half-frozen, they made a painful desert journey between November 15 and 19, and found themselves below the Hopi pueblo of Awatobi. Some seven hundred warriors emerged, armed and hostile. They shouted, they threw dust, some of the most audacious even rushed up to the Spaniards and snatched at their weapons; yet Vargas had ordered his men not to resist, and they remained calm no matter the provocation.

The pueblo's chief, who understood Spanish, appeared and conferred with Vargas. The governor explained that he had come in peace, and asked the chief to quiet his people. Though the chief attempted to restore order, the disturbance continued until Vargas, in high indignation, ordered the mob to kneel and beg forgiveness for their sins. "The crash of a thunderbolt would have left them less awe-struck than these words," says the *Mercurio Volante,* "and, having no answer to give, they laid down their arms and knelt on the ground to worship the Most Holy Mary in her image, striking their breasts many times. After this the Spaniards went on to the pueblo and entered what served as a public square, whose gateway permitted only one person to go in at a time, and that only by turning sidewise, and there they took possession of the town in the name of our king and Lord."

The next day the shattered church at Awatobi was re-dedicated and baptisms were held; Vargas stood as godfather for the grandchildren of the cacique. Then the Spaniards proceeded to the pueblo of Walpi, where the familiar scenes were enacted once more: a show of hostility by the Indians, a show of fearlessness by Vargas, and a bloodless capitulation of the village, followed by celebrations, feasting, and baptisms. Similar scenes took place at all the other Hopi towns, with the exception of Oraibi, the most distant one, which Vargas decided not to visit because of worsening weather and dwindling supplies. Oraibi sent word that it, too, submitted to the Spaniards, and that was sufficient for the moment. Vargas did lead his men part way to Oraibi for the purpose of investigating Toribio de la Huerta's alleged quicksilver mine; he found the outcroppings of reddish soil of which Huerta had spoken, and collected some samples, but it seemed doubtful to him that anything profitable would come from these deposits.

On November 24 Vargas took his leave of the Hopi chiefs and turned eastward. After rejoining the men he had left behind in Zuni country, Vargas set out on the return march to El Paso, taking a shortcut that an Indian guide showed them. They suffered severely from thirst and cold, and several times Apache attacked them, but did no harm. On December 10 the Spaniards reached the river near the ruined old pueblo of Socorro; the next day they passed the ruins of old Senecú, and on December 20, 1692, four months after they had gone forth to reconquer New Mexico, Vargas and his men made a triumphal entry into El Paso.

In those four months he had traversed nearly all of the inhabited region of New Mexico, and could claim that he had pacified and restored to loyalty a total of seventy-three pueblos.* This had been accomplished, he pointed out, without the loss of a single life, Spanish or native, for never once had he unsheathed his sword or fired a shot in battle. The friars had performed 2,214 baptisms and rededicated many desecrated churches. He had found the place of the reddish ore, and was forwarding samples to Mexico City for study. Peace had been restored; New Mexico was Spain's again.

* He was apparently including several dozen abandoned ones in this total.

10

The Reconquest Completed

THE 1692 Vargas expedition to New Mexico had been an extraordinary personal achievement. One can question the right of the Spaniards to claim the land of the Pueblos in the first place, but it is impossible to withhold admiration for the way Vargas reasserted Spain's authority there. Generosity and courtesy had proven more efficient than force and terror as methods of gaining power. The Indians with whom Vargas had been dealing were far from simple primitive folk; they were shrewd and intelligent, and they saw in this cool, far-sighted Spaniard a chance to escape the anarchy into which they had fallen after Popé's revolt. They had tried to govern themselves, and, to their despair, they had discovered that they no longer seemed capable of doing it. Now, exhausted, demoralized, sadly disunited, drained by years of foolish warfare of pueblo against pueblo, they had collapsed without a struggle in the face of Vargas' hypnotic fervor.

Vargas was aware of his own merits. In May, 1693, he wrote to the king to describe what he had done and to suggest some possible rewards that his Majesty might care to grant. First, he would like a title of nobility in Spain, specifically that of marquis of the Caramancheles, two towns near Madrid where his family owned land. Then, since he did not plan to remain in New Mexico past the time when the colony had been reestablished, he requested the office of captain-general and president of Guatemala. If this happened to be filled, he would be happy to accept the governorship of the Philippines, or else that of Chile, or, if nothing else was available, the governorship of what now is Argentina.

Whether the king was amused or annoyed by these requests, we do not know. The only fact that is certain is that none of them were granted; all Vargas received was a royal commendation. He was left with the governorship of New Mexico and nothing more, not even the title of nobility that he craved. Possibly the king had decided to wait and see how genuine the reconquest of New Mexico had been. All that glitters is not gold, nor even mercury, perhaps: the chemists in Mexico City had reported that Vargas' samples of reddish earth had been examined and had been found to have no quicksilver content.

Vargas spent the spring and summer of 1693 recruiting settlers for New Mexico and soldiers to protect them. "You might as well try to convert Jews without the Inquisition as Indians without soldiers," he told the Mexican viceroy. The viceroy set aside forty thousand pesos to pay the costs of assembling the army Vargas wanted, to the number of a hundred men. By mid-June he had his troops. From El Paso and surrounding New Biscay he managed to draw seventy families willing to take their chances on life in the north. A contingent of eighteen Franciscan friars enrolled to bring the Pueblos back to Christian ways. Several hundred Indian soldiers from the refugee pueblos around El Paso "volunteered," more or less willingly, to provide military support for the colonists.

On October 4, 1693, the colonizing expedition crossed the Rio Grande and began the trek up into New Mexico. Including the Indian allies, there were more than eight hundred people in the expedition; they had a thousand mules, nine hundred head of cattle, two thousand horses; their belongings were carried in eighteen wagons. Vargas, once again flying the yellow banner, rode ahead with a picked escort of soldiers to learn what he could about the mood in the pueblos.

What he found displeased him immensely. He had sent a friendly Indian from Zia to the Keresan pueblos with letters announcing his return; the scout came back to say that in nearly every village last year's pledges of allegiance had been forgotten the moment the Spaniards left New Mexico. In Cochiti, Santo Domingo, and most of the others the Indians suspected that Vargas would go back on his word, and planned to punish them for their part in the 1680 revolt; they intended to resist a new Spanish settlement. Of the Keresan group only the pueblos of San Felipe and Santa Ana seemed ready to welcome the Spaniards; Zia was undecided, though leaning away from the side of hostility. If Vargas proposed to plant a colony in the land, he realized, he would probably have to fight to do it.

With these unhappy tidings he rode back to join the main column of the expedition, and discovered that thirty women and children had died crossing a harsh stretch of the desert long known as the Dead Man's March. The rest moved slowly northward toward Santa Fe. En route, messengers arrived from Pecos with word that that pueblo was loyal and would offer aid to the Spaniards. Vargas sent the always useful Bartolomé de Ojeda, who had accompanied him, off to Zia under instructions to remind his people of their oaths. Other messengers went to the Tewa and Tano villages of the north in the hope of regaining the friendship of these Indians and their powerful chieftain Tupatú, who in Vargas' absence seems to have had second thoughts about his pro-Spanish position.

On December 16 the colonists reached Santa Fe. They found the Tano inhabitants of the city polite but cool. Unsmilingly the Indians allowed Vargas, his soldiers, and the friars to enter, and without much enthusiasm they provided a modest supply of corn for the Spaniards. Vargas explained to the Indians that it was not Spain's intention to take from them anything that was rightfully theirs; but Santa Fe, he said, had been founded as a Spanish city, and now he would have to ask the Indians living there to return to their old villages in the Galisteo region. The Tanos looked at him blankly, as though they could not understand what he was telling them.

Sensing problems, Vargas decided not to force the issue. For the time being he would leave the Indians in possession of the city; he had his colonists make camp in the fields outside Santa Fe while he tried to persuade the natives to depart peacefully. But the Indians showed no desire to withdraw. More than a week went by; the Spaniards, huddling in freezing tents, suffered in the snow, and twenty-two children died of the cold. There were more signs of independence from the Indians, who declined to supply more corn, or to bring timber for the repair of Santa Fe's church. From some of the northern pueblos, now, came suspicious-sounding requests that priests immediately be sent to them; but the friars, fearing murder, did not want to be scattered throughout the land until the capital had been reoccupied, and Vargas granted their petition against going to the pueblos just yet.

Finally, though eager to avoid armed conflict, Vargas

came to the limits of his patience. His people could not camp in the snow any longer. Bluntly he ordered the Tanos to leave Santa Fe; they responded, on December 28, by closing the entrance to the plaza and taking up defensive positions along the walls. War now was inevitable. Vargas summoned 140 Indian troops from Pecos and stormed the city on the 29th.

The siege lasted all day; arrows, stones, and boiling water showered down from the walls on the attackers. The Spaniards broke through the gate, then had to pull back in order to drive off reinforcements sent by the Tewa pueblos. When night came the Tanos still held the capital, but they had suffered heavy casualties in the battle, and their wounded chief had hanged himself. In the morning they surrendered. This time Vargas made no pretense of kindliness: seventy of the Indian leaders were immediately executed. Thus he served notice to all of New Mexico that he would tolerate no breaches of 1692's promises of loyalty. His own losses had been light; one Spaniard and five warriors from Pecos had been killed in the attack.

Santa Fe was again a Spanish city, but it had been won at the cost of Vargas' policy of peaceful reconciliation. As 1694 began, the colonists found themselves isolated in a wintry, hostile land. Pecos, Zia, Santa Ana, and San Felipe remained friendly, but the other pueblos had reverted to rebelliousness, and Vargas saw that he would have to reconquer them one by one, doing anew the work of 1692, if the colony was to survive.

A major center of resistance was the Tewa pueblo of San Ildefonso, north of the capital. Here had gathered the people of half a dozen Tewa towns, along with Tanos from San Cristóbal and San Lázaro, to plot the overthrow of the Spaniards. On January 9 Vargas marched to the Black Mesa, near

San Ildefonso, where his foes had assembled; he made the customary offers of peace and pardons, but received only vague answers, obviously designed to create delay while the Indians made alliances with the other unfriendly tribes. Three weeks later Vargas went back to the Black Mesa to repeat his offers; this time the natives suggested that they would submit if Vargas and a friar, and no one else, entered their camp. Such feats of bravery had worked for Vargas in 1692, but now, realizing that he would almost certainly be slain, he did not take the risk.

In the weeks that followed Vargas frequently sent messengers to the rebels, but his friendly overtures were met with reminders of the seventy Tanos who had been shot after the surrender of Santa Fe. Meanwhile the Spaniards searched gloomily for a lead mine so that they could increase their meager stock of ammunition, and watched as their supplies of food dwindled. Vargas was forced to send out raiding parties to capture corn from nearby pueblos; the Indians began to destroy their surpluses rather than let them fall to the Spaniards. There were rumors of a joint attack by Tewas, Tanos, Apache, and warriors from the western pueblos. Time seemed to be on the Indians' side. The Spaniards would have to take the offensive or perish.

On March 4, 1694, with about sixty soldiers, thirty members of Santa Fe's civilian militia, and a large number of Pecos allies, Vargas attacked the mesa at San Ildefonso. Rain and snow hampered the charging Spaniards, and the rebels held firm during a five-hour battle: fifteen of Vargas' Indians were killed and twenty Spaniards were wounded, eight of them seriously. It was the worst defeat the Spaniards had known since the revolt itself, and it badly damaged their morale. Obtaining reinforcements, Vargas pursued the attack on San Ildefonso from March 11 to 19, but bad weather and stubborn defense kept the Spaniards at bay, and finally they had to withdraw, having accomplished nothing except to seize a large quantity of corn.

Then came word from the friendly Keresan pueblos, Zia, Santa Ana, and San Felipe, that the other Keresan villages of Cochiti and Santo Domingo were plotting an attack on the Spaniards and their allies. The conspirators had assembled at a mesa called La Cieneguilla near Cochiti, where the Santo Domingo people had settled after returning from the western hills. On April 17, Vargas attacked La Cieneguilla with the aid of a detachment of friendly Keresans commanded by Bartolomé de Ojeda of Zia. Dividing his troops into three columns, Vargas executed a classic offensive maneuver that allowed him to surround and surprise his enemy with total success. Many Indians were killed, hundreds of women and children were taken prisoner, and the Spaniards burned the pueblo after removing its grain and livestock. In part payment for their help, Vargas gave his Indian allies two hundred head of cattle.

In May the loyal Indians made war against Jemez, another center of anti-Spanish feeling, but could not defeat the rebels. Meanwhile Vargas and his people stayed close to Santa Fe, trying to strengthen their precarious position and make a start at raising crops. Food continued to be a problem for them, and at the end of June Vargas led a small raiding expedition north to Taos, which was said to have a good stock of corn. The Indians of Taos fled into a nearby canyon, shrewdly leaving crosses raised in their pueblo in the hope that the Spaniards would respect their property. This gambit succeeded at first; but after Vargas failed to persuade the Indians to return to their village to negotiate with him, he confiscated as much of their corn as his mules could carry, and burned the rest.

Next he moved against Jemez. On July 24 he mounted a surprise attack with 120 Spaniards and, once again, a force of Keresans under Bartolomé de Ojeda. Without Ojeda's help, it is doubtful that the Spaniards would have maintained themselves in New Mexico through 1694, just as they could not have survived 1692 without the support of Tupatú. Thus did the Indians themselves, by placing tribal rivalries above their common interest, make possible the reconquest of New Mexico. With warriors from Zia and Santa Ana playing an important part, Vargas' force attacked Jemez from two sides at once and inflicted a bloody defeat: eighty-four Jemez Indians lost their lives, and almost four hundred were captured. On the Spanish side there were no fatalities, although many were wounded. The cattle and corn of Jemez were taken, most of it being distributed to Vargas' Indian allies, and the pueblo was set afire. A few days later, the remaining leaders of Jemez came to Vargas to ask for pardon, blaming their rebelliousness on the influence of a single chief, whom they were willing to surrender. Vargas took the chief into custody and sentenced him to death, but, when his people asked for mercy, the governor commuted the sentence to one of ten years' labor in the mines of New Biscay. Jemez then once again submitted to Spanish authority.

Now only one area of trouble remained along the Rio Grande: San Ildefonso. Rebels from nine Tewa and Tano pueblos still were camped on the Black Mesa, periodically descending to raid Santa Fe's outskirts. At the beginning of September, 1694, Vargas assembled all the available Spanish fighting men and his allies from Pecos, Zia, Santa Ana, and San Felipe. Even Jemez contributed warriors when Vargas agreed to release his remaining Jemez prisoners in return for their services. On September 4 this large army attacked the mesa, but the charge was poorly coordinated and was repulsed, as was a smaller-scale attack the next day. Conceding that the mesa could not be stormed, Vargas laid seige to it, and for the next few days the defenders were treated to the sight of the Spaniards destroying the nearly ripened corn in the fields below their eyrie. This infuriated and then disheartened them, and, after several minor skirmishes, they began to ask for peace on September 8.

Thus the year's warfare ended. It had been a dreary, bitter business for Vargas, a sad contrast to the glorious cavalcade of 1692. Indians and Spaniards had perished in battle; pueblos had been sacked; crops had been destroyed; new chasms of mistrust had opened between white man and native. But what choice had there been? He had brought his people into a land that he thought had been pacified, and when it proved to be not entirely hospitable to the settlers, he had had to make war. Like Oñate a century earlier, he had begun with high ideals, and had been compelled by the necessities of the situation to deal more harshly with the Pueblos as time went on.

But Vargas was not Oñate, and, with a shaky peace restored, he set about reviving 1692's spirit of harmony. From September to December of 1694 he toured the villages, attempting to demonstrate his concern for the natives' welfare even as he reestablished the structure of Spanish governmental control over them. He checked on the condition of each pueblo, the state of its fields and food supplies, the equipment its people might need. At the same time he saw to it that native governors, judges, and sheriffs were once again appointed in the villages to serve as the instruments of Spanish authority. Churches and missions were rebuilt, and by the end of the year the friars were again at work throughout the valley. The Spaniards had learned one sober lesson from the revolt of 1680, though: Christianity could not be forced upon the Indians. The new missionaries resigned themselves to the fact that the kiva and the church would have to be allowed to exist side by side.

Seventy families of new settlers arrived from Mexico in the spring of 1695. They founded a new town called Santa Cruz in April, near the site of a short-lived pre-revolt settlement of the same name. Unfortunately, the land assigned to the Santa Cruz settlers already belonged to the Indians of San Cristóbal and San Lázaro, who were forced to move elsewhere. This created unnecessary new tensions. Downriver, some of the old haciendas were reoccupied, although Vargas was careful not to revive the discredited encomienda system that had made virtual slaves of the Indians. The former hacienda of the Bernal family blossomed into a town, Bernalillo, just across the ruins of the pueblo of Puaray, where Coronado had made his winter camp more than 150 years earlier.

"With full sails we forge ahead," Vargas wrote to the viceroy. But, though Spaniards again farmed the land of New Mexico and Pueblo Indians again studied the language, religion, and technology of the white men, the colony's situation was far from ideal. The peace was fragile; discontented Indians still muttered about rebellion, and the Spaniards knew it. The expansion of the new Spanish farms was slow, so that the settlers were a long way from being self-supporting. The climate was still one of drought, and the Apache were as troublesome as ever.

A poor harvest in the autumn of 1695 intensified the difficulties for Indians and settlers alike. That winter famine oppressed all of New Mexico; according to one possibly exaggerated account, the Spaniards were forced to eat dogs, cats, horses, mules, bull-hides, even old bones, then started chewing weeds in the fields, and many died of starvation.

The mood of the natives grew surlier as their sufferings increased, and whispers of revolt were heard in several villages. In March, 1696, the father-president warned Vargas that trouble was near, and asked that soldiers be posted at each mission to guard against a repetition of the massacre of 1680. But Vargas could not believe such things would happen again, and did not care to make his regime seem oppressive to the natives by sending troops into the villages. Hinting broadly that he thought the dangers were imaginary and the missionaries were perhaps letting themselves be frightened too easily, he invited any friar who felt endangered to move to Santa Fe. Though some of them accepted the offer, most, their pride stung, remained on duty in the pueblos; five friars thus met martyrdom when the new uprising broke out on June 4, 1696.

The pueblos that rebelled were Taos, Picuris, Cochiti, Santo Domingo, Jemez, and a number of the Tewa and Tano villages. The friars at Taos, Jemez, San Ildefonso, Nambé, and San Cristóbal were put to death; 21 Spanish soldiers and settlers also lost their lives; each of the rebellious towns desecrated and burned its church.

Once again sudden violence had seared the Spanish colony in New Mexico. But this revolt, though it stirred horrifying memories of 1680, was not the universal catastrophe that that earlier upheaval had been. Pecos, Tesuque, San Felipe, Santa Ana, and Zia remained faithful to Spain. There was no attack on Santa Fe or any of the outlying Spanish settlements. The Indians of the affected pueblos did not even attempt to maintain their independence on their home grounds: immediately after the slaughter of the friars they abandoned their villages. Some fled to the west and took refuge among the Zuni, Hopi, or Ácoma people; the others hid in the hills flanking the Rio Grande and prepared to conduct guerrilla warfare against the Spaniards from there.

In planning his response to the disturbance, Vargas' first move was to take stock of his Indian allies. From Zia came a report from Bartolomé de Ojeda: Jemez had attacked his pueblo to punish it for its sympathies to the Spaniards, but the attackers had been driven off and Ojeda had raided Jemez in return. "As you know," Ojeda told Vargas, "we are on the frontier, and I beg of you to send me firearms, powder, and bullets, for you know well that we are very loyal vassals of His Majesty." Vargas sent a request to Pecos for assistance, and on June 7 the governor of that pueblo arrived at Santa Fe with a hundred mounted warriors. Other loyal pueblos pledged troops also.

During the first weeks after the uprising Vargas deliberately launched no major campaign against the rebels. They had deserted their homes in late spring, leaving their young crops untended; he wanted them now to worry about the growing corn, to grow tense and uneasy in their mountain hideouts, before he struck at them. Psychological warfare was his specialty: he preferred to fight a worried, hungry foe than a fiery, defiant one.

Only a few minor skirmishes took place, then. In one of them the chief of Santo Domingo, a leader of the rebellion, was captured. Vargas had him executed on June 14. At the end of June, with sixty Spanish soldiers and his Pecos allies, Vargas shifted his headquarters from Santa Fe to the new town of Santa Cruz, from which he could control the entire Tano-Tewa district. Thus he was able to keep many of the rebels penned up in the mountains while their neglected crops perished and their food supplies shrank. Starvation and crumbling morale soon forced the Tewas and Tanos to surrender; they came out of the hills, won Vargas' pardon, and returned to their villages. When one Indian of the Tewa town of Nambé was asked why the revolt had broken out, he said it was because "a Spaniard had remarked, while in Cochiti, that the governor of New Mexico was planning to kill all the adult men of the pueblos, sparing only the boys." No one could trace the source of this wild and provocative rumor.

Despite the severe economic pressure Vargas was applying, the Tiwas of Picuris refused to yield—perhaps because their chieftains, Luis and Lorenzo Tupatú, were afraid to face Vargas after having betrayed their allegiance to him. Instead of coming out of the hills, the Picuris folk fled through the mountains to the uninhabited country north of Taos. This proved to be a mistake: the entire tribe fell into the hands of the Apache, and spent ten years living as captives in western Kansas before being rescued by a Spanish expedition in 1706.

Having restored order along the Rio Grande without a single real battle, Vargas swung westward. On July 23 he attacked and smashed a mixed force of Indians from Jemez, Ácoma, and Zuni, and six days later he defeated the remnants of this group, both times inflicting heavy losses while suffering just a few casualties. Early in August he laid siege to Ácoma, but failed to gain access to the mesa-top, and had to be content with ravaging the cornfields below. Then he returned to Santa Cruz, and in September, aided by troops from Pecos and Tesuque, he marched to Taos. The Indians of this village were barricaded in a canyon east of their pueblo, as they had been many times before; Vargas devastated their fields and after about a week they chose to surrender.

By the end of 1696, the last of the Pueblo rebellions was over. Armed resistance to Spanish rule along the Rio Grande had ended for all time. Disease, drought, and civil strife had weakened the Indians disastrously; the constant abandonment and rebuilding of their pueblos had drained their energy almost beyond the point where it could be replenished; and the shrewd military tactics of Diego de Vargas had completed the process of exhaustion. Thereafter they would live peacefully in their villages, isolated pockets of an older culture in the midst of the rapidly growing Spanish civilization of New Mexico. Only in the western territories did they maintain their independence, for the Spaniards had never exerted any significant control over Ácoma, Zuni, or the Hopi pueblos, and Vargas wisely did not try to extend his administration into that region now. Those Indians of the Rio Grande district who could not abide living under Spanish rule moved westward. Refugees from Cochiti and Santo Domingo founded the new Keresan pueblo of Laguna, near Ácoma. Some rebellious Tewas from San Ildefonso and other villages went all the way to the Hopi country, where they were allowed to settle on First Mesa. Their descendents still live there, alongside the Hopi pueblos, in the Tewa-speaking town of Hano.

Vargas, by this time, seems to have abandoned his hopes of winning a governorship in the Philippines, Guatemala, Chile, or any other part of Spain's empire more promising than New Mexico. Having brought New Mexico back to life and seen it through its difficult early years of resettlement, he was willing and eager now to preside over its coming era of recovery and prosperity. Its farms again were thriving, its population was increasing, the Indians no longer posed any threat. Through a network of personal friendships with Bartolomé de Ojeda and other loyal Pueblos, Vargas had built up an army of Indian auxiliary troops far larger than any force of Spaniards he could have recruited, and felt confident that a recurrence of the old conflicts was impossible.

Under his leadership Spaniards and Indians would move forward together toward a happy, flourishing life.

His five-year term as governor expired in 1696. Believing that his work in New Mexico was just beginning, Vargas asked the king to grant him a second term. He assumed that the reappointment would come through as a matter of course; but it was always dangerous to assume that the Spanish government would act in a rational manner. While Vargas' application was making its way slowly up the channels of the Madrid bureaucracy, a certain Don Pedro Rodríguez Cubero requested of the king that New Mexico be turned over to him. For some reason the king agreed, and in the spring of 1697 Governor Vargas was notified that Cubero would shortly arrive in Santa Fe as his replacement.

Vargas was astounded. Who was this outsider? How could a stranger possibly understand what tact, what delicacy, must be displayed to guarantee future Indian cooperation? Why such an ungrateful removal from office just as the first rewards of these years of labor could be glimpsed? Vargas appealed to the viceroy and to the king, but it did no good; he was caught in the wheels of the system, and when Cubero entered Santa Fe on July 2, 1697, it was necessary for Vargas to stand down.

His sense of propriety would not allow him to make a public issue of what he considered this unreasonable and unjustified dismissal. Obediently, he turned the palace of the governors over to his successor, and promised to do whatever he could to insure a smooth transition for the incoming administration. Now a private citizen, Vargas took up humbler lodgings in Santa Fe; he could not leave New Mexico until the new governor had completed the customary investigation into the outgoing governor's conduct while in office.

For several months this routine inquiry droned along.

Suddenly, on October 2, a squad of soldiers called on Vargas and informed him that he was under arrest, by order of Governor Cubero. He was taken to a small cell at one end of the palace where for five years he had ruled as governor; placed in solitary confinement, he was denied the right to notify Spain or Mexico City of his imprisonment, or even to communicate with his friends in Santa Fe.

The town council of the capital now drew up a list of charges against Vargas. An astonishing number of secret enemies came forward to accuse him of mismanagement. Those who resented his unwillingness to grant Indian land to Spaniards, those who felt he had paid insufficient heed to the suggestions of his subordinates, those who merely envied him for his grace and intelligence and wealth, hastened to denounce him. He was charged with having embezzled money set aside for the recruiting of colonists; with having provoked all the uprisings of 1694–96 by ordering the execution of the seventy Tano captives after the seizure of Santa Fe; with having received supplies from Mexico and selling them for his own profit; and many other things.

The accusations ranged from exaggerations to outright lies. But Vargas swiftly was found guilty, and Cubero levied a heavy sentence. The former governor was fined four thousand pesos and all his property in New Mexico was confiscated; and he was sent back to his cell in the palace for what was apparently intended as an indefinite prison term. With bewildering speed, then, had Vargas come to a total downfall in 1697—from conquering hero to helpless prisoner in less than six months.

At one end of the palace, now, Governor Cubero scribbled endless official documents and, so it was whispered, indulged rather too much in wine, while at the other end Vargas endured month after month of dismal confinement, cut off from contact with everyone except the jailers who brought him his food. The colonists came to accept the strange state of affairs, and, though Cubero seems to have been barely competent as an administrator, New Mexico somehow continued to thrive on the momentum Vargas had supplied. By the end of 1697 there were more than three hundred families in the colony, and the total Spanish population exceeded fifteen hundred, the highest figure since 1680. There were no further difficulties with the Indians, and the last holdouts among the rebels decided to drop their pose of hostility: Ácoma, Zuni, and the new Laguna pueblo all made formal acts of submission to the government at Santa Fe, leaving only the Hopi independent.

Through 1698 and 1699 there were signs of a decline in the vigor of the colony, though. The Indian allies, who could not comprehend the dismissal of the heroic Vargas, lost interest in patrolling the borders of the Spanish settlements, and some of the more remote new towns and haciendas had to be abandoned. The Spanish soldiers, uninspired by Cubero's leadership, grew indifferent also; there were numerous desertions. While Cubero prepared lengthy reports in triplicate and quadruplicate, farm production fell off, buildings went unrepaired, and a general air of demoralization settled over New Mexico. During this time Vargas remained in his cell, a forgotten figure.

At the beginning of 1700 came a tentative move toward an expansion of Spanish authority. For the first time in twenty years, a missionary dared to visit the Hopi—a friar named Juan Garaycoechea, who went to Awatobi, the easternmost Hopi village, and converted seventy-three of its people to Christianity.

One of the darkest episodes in Pueblo history followed. The people of the other Hopi towns, angered by the hospitality shown to the friar, resolved that Awatobi must be destroyed. At dawn one day soon after Fray Juan's departure, a Hopi war party climbed the mesa on which Awatobi was situated. A man of the pueblo who opposed the return of Christianity opened the sturdy wooden door that was the only entrance to the village. The attackers burst in. They found many of the men of Awatobi in the kiva, and set it afire, leaving them trapped in the flames. Then the invaders raced through the village, striking down anyone they found. Only a few women and girls were spared—just those who had not been baptized, and who were able to recite the prayers of the native religion. By the time the sun rose, Awatobi looked like a slaughterhouse. The surviving women were carried away to other pueblos. The attackers finished their work by despoiling the village itself, tearing down walls, smashing pottery, shattering looms. Awatobi was left in ruins, and was never reoccupied. The doom of Awatobi kept Christianity out of the Hopi pueblos for more than a century thereafter.

In May, 1700, a few months after the massacre, a Hopi delegation came to Santa Fe to propose a peace treaty, the main provision of which would have allowed the Hopi to retain their own religion even after coming under Spanish authority. Governor Cubero rejected this, and the delegates went back to their mesas; Hopi independence would continue for the next 150 years.

In 1700, also, the unfortunate Vargas finally found an ally. The father-president of the Franciscan missions in New Mexico went to Mexico City to inform the viceroy of what had befallen the deposed governor. The viceroy was appalled, and ordered Vargas to be released instantly, pending a full investigation of his case.

In July, 1700, Vargas set out for Mexico City to seek

justice. When he arrived, he learned that he had been the victim of a bureaucratic misunderstanding: the king had been willing all along to grant him a second term as governor, but had been under the impression that Vargas did not want reappointment, and had given the post to Cubero. By the time the king had become aware of Vargas' application, it was thought to be too late to withdraw Cubero's appointment. However, by a letter of June 15, 1699, the king had expressed his gratitude to the viceroy for Vargas' past services, and had issued instructions that Vargas was to be made governor again upon the expiration of Cubero's term in 1702, or earlier if the office became vacant before then. In addition, Vargas was to be offered a title of nobility, and was asked to inform the king whether he preferred to be a marquis or a count.

The viceroy had not been able to forward any of this happy news to Vargas at Santa Fe, for, during the three years of Vargas' imprisonment, no one in Mexico had any idea where the former governor was. Only now, released at last from his confinement, could he be told of the high honors that had been conferred on him.

Vargas remained in Mexico City until he had completely cleared himself of the charges that had been lodged against him. He was in no hurry to return to Santa Fe; perhaps he wished to spend some time amid the luxuries of the Mexican capital, after so long a time in a jail cell, before going back to the spartan life of the northern colony. Not until July, 1703, did Vargas—now the Marquis of La Nava Brazinas—depart for New Mexico. Cubero, hearing that the man he had succeeded and jailed was on his way back to succeed him, speedily packed his belongings and left Santa Fe, letting it be known that he was going off to fight the Apache. He was never seen in New Mexico again.

In November, 1703, the Marquis of La Nava Brazinas entered Santa Fe and graciously accepted the homage of the same officials who had sent him to prison six years before. "It is justice which I ask," he told them, and called for a review of all the charges that had been lodged against him. One by one he demonstrated their falsity, and nobody dared contradict his testimony. The accusations, the town council obligingly ruled, had been "made up, hatched, and invented" by the vanished Cubero, and Vargas was provided with a document declaring his full innocence.

Then he commenced an investigation into Cubero's administration of the colony. Vargas found little to praise in that: the army had gone to pieces, the fields were full of weeds, everything seemed to be crumbling. It seemed to him that Cubero had tried "to destroy all I had done and leave no memory of it." The town council agreed, declaring that Vargas, by his "ability and resolution," had restored New Mexico to Spain, and that Cubero had let everything fall apart, which could only be explained "by the great enmity and disaffection he has toward the said Lord Marquis, trying by every means to show his malice. . . ." The officials who had served in Cubero's government now signed an affidavit stating that the former governor "was solely occupied in drinking and writing papers with no reason whatever," and in "imagining things he had no business to imagine, ascribing faults and crimes to those who had not committed them, like that which he attributed to the said Lord Marquis."

Injustice had been undone. Now there was work to do— repairs to make, enemies to defeat. The Indians of the Rio Grande pueblos were peaceful, purged forever by repeated defeat of the hunger for revolt, but the Apache were an unending problem. They still came swooping out of the mountains flanking the central valley and ripped through the haciendas, stealing livestock and produce. Cubero had planned several punitive expeditions against them, but he had never managed to accomplish anything. Early in 1704 the settlers around Bernalillo advised Vargas of their difficulties and begged him to make war against the Apache "with fire and sword." He pledged that he would, and began assembling his army.

The Marquis of La Nava Brazinas was now sixty-one years old. Twelve years had passed since his bloodless march through rebellious New Mexico, when he had said outside Santa Fe, "He who takes no risks to win an immortal name accomplishes nothing." Eight years had gone by since he last had led troops at all. He had spent three of those years in a cramped cell. Yet he did not hesitate to don his old armor when the need came.

With forty-seven Spaniards, both soldiers and settlers, he marched downriver to Bernalillo on March 27, 1704. There he was joined by 120 Pueblo troops, for this was to be a joint effort of Spaniards and Indians against a common foe. The roster of Indian allies tells us how thoroughly the Pueblos had been integrated into the life of the colony, for they came from a dozen villages, many of them once bitterly hostile to the Spaniards: Cochiti, San Ildefonso, Santo Domingo, San Juan, Santa Clara, Tesuque, San Felipe, Pecos, Jemez, Zia, Santa Ana, Nambé. On March 30 scouts went eastward into the mountains to look for the Apache; the next day they were observed at a watering place at the edge of the Plain of the Inferno, and on April 2 Vargas led the main body of his army toward them. But as the trail went upward into the Manzanos Mountains, Vargas felt discomfort in the thin air; he was strangely weak, with a fever and pains in his chest. He tried to go on. A day later, though, he was too weak even to make his regular journal entry on the progress of the campaign, and his officers told him that he must not continue, that he had to return to Bernalillo until he was well. Reluctantly he gave in, and let himself be taken to the settlement on the river, to the hacienda of Bernalillo's mayor, Don Fernando Durán y Chaves. There he rested for a few days, waiting for his strength to rise, until he realized that it was not going to rise, and on April 7 he sent for his secretary in order to dictate his last will.

"In the name of God almighty," he began, and asked "a most clear career of salvation" for his soul, while offering his body "to the earth from which it was made." He gave instructions for his funeral, and for the division of his property. To his two sons, his armor, his shirts of Dutch linen, "embroidered with the best of lace," his fine suits of court dress, his plumed hats, his French cloaks, his leather boots, his pistols, his swords. To his daughter, a substantial cash sum, to be raised by selling his diamond rings, his earrings set with emeralds and pearls, his silver plates and tankards and forks and spoons. He gave money also to his servants, and ordered his two slaves to be freed, and left funds to the church to pay the costs of saying two hundred masses for himself, and three hundred "for the souls of the poor who died in the conquest of this kingdom." He asked to be buried in Santa Fe. By now pneumonia gripped his chest and he could barely speak; he made an end of his testament and signed it, "The Marquis de la Brazinas." On April 8, 1704, he died and was taken back to the capital for burial, and on the day of his funeral fifty measures of corn and twelve head of cattle were given in his name to the poor of Santa Fe; and there were Indians as well as Spaniards among his mourners.

With Vargas the heroic age of Spanish conquest in the New World ended. He had been born after his time, for if he had been a sixteenth-century man he might have mastered some golden kingdom of South America, but by his day there was nothing left to take but a windswept, desert plateau north of the Rio Grande. He brought an age to its close, for after him the empire of Spain decayed and slowly fell apart; but at least he was, unlike most of the earlier conquistadores in and out of New Mexico, a man worth mourning.

The time when Pueblo chiefs might plot to regain their freedom was gone, too. There still were anti-Spanish factions, particularly at Pecos and San Juan, but they did nothing but murmur and mutter, and gradually the Pueblos settled down under Spanish control. Instead of fighting the Spaniards, they joined with them to fight the Apache and Navajo, the enemies of the cultivated fields. They went to their churches to worship the Christian god, and then they went to their kivas to pray in the old manner, and as the years passed the last few died away who could still remember the grave moment of the 1680 uprising.

As Spanish towns spread up and down the valley of the Rio Grande, the Pueblo Indians seemed to fade from the world. The Spaniards brought them such gifts as measles and smallpox, which took hundreds of lives; some of them left their pueblos to settle among the white folk, and were lost forever to their tribes; others vanished into the camps of the Apache. Zia, which had had more than 2,000 inhabitants at the time of the revolt, had just 568 in 1760, and 275 in 1793. The population of San Ildefonso fell from 900 to 484 between 1700 and 1765, then dropped to 225 by the end of the eighteenth century. In the eighteenth century Picuris dwindled from 2,500 to 200; Pecos became a ghost town, abandoned altogether by 1838; nearly all the other pueblos lost at least half their pre-revolt populations, while the Spaniards were increasing during the eighteenth century to

20,000. By the 1790's there were four Spanish towns in the valley with populations of more than 2,000—Santa Fe, Santa Cruz, Albuquerque, and El Paso—and many smaller towns.

In the west, where the intrusion of the Spaniards could not be blamed for the disruption of Indian life, the story was much the same. A priest who visited the Hopi in 1776 took a census and counted 7,494 of them in five villages. Then drought and plague struck. No rain fell for three years. A Spanish expedition in 1780 found only 798 Hopi alive; in the previous four years, nine out of every ten had died. Of 30,000 sheep, only 300 remained. There were five horses, no cattle.

The eighteenth century was the low point for the Indians, though, and the high point for the Spaniards. Slowly the Indian populations rose again. Meanwhile Spain lost her grip on the New World; in 1822 Mexico won her independence and the pueblos passed from Spanish to Mexican control. That in itself did not make much difference. The western pueblos still were outside the sphere of European settlement, and those of the Rio Grande continued to struggle along, more troubled by the Apache and Navajo than by the white men. But New Mexico was not destined to remain a Mexican province for long. The young, adventurous United States of America was looking westward. Traders had opened the Santa Fe trail, and furs, gold, and silver were traveling along it to the rich cities of the east. The United States talked of a "manifest destiny" to expand from coast to coast, and Mexico stood in the way.

In 1846 President Polk declared war against Mexico. The Mexican War is not the noblest episode in American history; it amounted to little more than an unabashed grab of a neighboring country's territory. But "manifest destiny" would not be denied. On August 18, 1846, General Stephen Watts

Kearny entered Santa Fe and raised the American flag without firing a shot. The conquest was confirmed in 1848 by the Treaty of Guadalupe Hidalgo, in which Mexico was compelled to yield to the United States the vast territory now comprising the states of New Mexico, Arizona, Utah, Nevada, and California, receiving in return the modest sum of fifteen million dollars.

There was one flicker of Indian defiance as New Mexico passed into the hands of the United States. The Mexican authorities in New Mexico succeeded in persuading some Taos Indians that the Americans would rule them oppressively; in January, 1847, these Indians burst into the house of the newly appointed American governor, Charles Bent, killing him and several other men. A brief anti-American revolt swept through New Mexico, but the Indians quickly surrendered when American troops moved against them.

The Pueblos now came under United States administration. They became the responsibility of the Bureau of Indian Affairs, part of the War Department. They caused no further problems. "A more upright and useful people are nowhere to be found," wrote a nineteenth-century government agent at Santa Fe. The Americans brought the Apache and Navajo under control, opened schools and hospitals for the Indians, and set aside reservations so that there would be no further intrusions on their land. Today there are more than 25,000 Pueblo Indians living in and about the eighteen New Mexican pueblos, and the population is growing by nearly a thousand every year. In Arizona are about five thousand Hopi on a 631,000-acre reservation completely surrounded by the huge reservation of the settled, prosperous Navajo. They still live in their dusty, mid-walled villages, but television aerials sprout from the flat roofs, and shiny automobiles are parked in the narrow streets.

Human history is an archive of conquests. In the past five hundred years, particularly, the men of Europe have spilled forth to the other continents, coolly claiming land that other men thought they owned. They have set up governments, founded churches, ordered changes in styles of dress, and generally transformed the lives of those unfortunate enough to stand in the way of expanding empires.

Occasionally—not often—the victims of progress have succeeded in driving back the intruders who would seize their world. The Pueblo Revolt of 1680 was one such moment of success. As we have seen, it was hardly a brilliant victory, for the Indians were attacking an outnumbered and enfeebled band of uncertain colonists; and even that humble triumph was shortlived. The white man's touch had ruined the Pueblo Indians in only eighty years, leaving them incapable of governing themselves. Their return to independence, so unusual in the story of the American Indian, was soured by tribal rivalry, and they laid down their freedom almost gladly once a conqueror of the quality of Vargas appeared.

Why was it necessary for the Spaniards to have the Indians' land? Why could the men of Spain not have stayed in their own place, leaving the Pueblos to theirs? The Indians asked those questions frequently, and still do. The white men could not offer proper answers, for how could one explain to an Indian such concepts as the divinely inspired need to spread Christianity, or the dynamic nature of an empire-building nation, which must forever thrust outward, or the white man's mission to bring civilization to savages? The Indian would merely say to such elaborate philosophical notions that they were high-flown ways of disguising greed. You came to steal our land because you wanted it, they would say. We do not know why you wanted it, since it was not of great use to you, but you came, and stole. That is all that matters.

And if we could have flung you back to the place from which you came, we would have done it. We tried; for a little while we succeeded; then we failed. And here are we, and here are you, and who knows why such things must be? And that is all.

Bibliography

Bailey, J. B. *Diego de Vargas and the Reconquest of New Mexico*. Albuquerque: University of New Mexico Press, 1940.

Bancroft, H. H. *History of Arizona and New Mexico, 1530–1888*. San Francisco: The History Company, 1889. Reissued, 1962 (Albuquerque: Horn & Wallace).

————. *History of Mexico*. San Francisco: A. L. Bancroft & Co., 1883–1888.

Bolton, H. E. *The Spanish Borderlands: A Chronicle of Old Florida and the Southwest*. New Haven: Yale University Press, 1921.

————, editor. *Spanish Exploration in the Southwest, 1542–1706*. New York: Scribner, 1908. Reissued, 1963 (New York: Barnes & Noble).

Chapman, Walker. *The Golden Dream: Seekers of El Dorado*. New York: Bobbs-Merrill, 1967.

Espinosa, J. M. *Crusaders of the Rio Grande: The Story of Don Diego de Vargas*. Chicago: Institute of Jesuit History, 1942.

————. *First Expedition of Vargas into New Mexico, 1692*. Albuquerque: University of New Mexico Press, 1940.

Hackett, C. W. "The Causes for the Failure of Otermín's Attempt to Reconquer New Mexico, 1681–1682." In *Pacific Ocean in History*. New York: Panama-Pacific Historical Congress, 1917.

————, editor. *Revolt of the Pueblo Indians of New Mexico and Otermín's Attempted Reconquest, 1680–1682*. Albuquerque: University of New Mexico Press, 1942.

Horgan, Paul. *Conquistadors in North America*. London: Macmillan & Co., 1963.

——. *Great River: The Rio Grande in North American History*. New York: Rinehart & Co., 1954.

Jones, Oakah L., Jr. *Pueblo Warriors and Spanish Conquest*. Norman: University of Oklahoma Press, 1966.

Josephy, Alvin M., Jr. *The Patriot Chiefs: A Chronicle of American Indian Leadership*. New York: The Viking Press, 1961.

Kidder, Alfred Vincent. *An Introduction to the Study of Southwestern Archaeology*. New Haven: Yale University Press, 1924, 1962.

Siguenza y Góngora, Don Carlos de. *The Mercurio Volante*. Edited by Irving Albert Leonard. Los Angeles: The Quivira Society, 1932.

Silverberg, Robert. *The Old Ones: Indians of the American Southwest*. Greenwich, Connecticut: New York Graphic Society, 1965.

Spicer, Edward H. *Cycles of Conquest: The Impact of Spain, Mexico, and the United States on the Indians of the Southwest, 1533–1960*. Tucson: University of Arizona Press, 1962.

Villagrá, Gaspar Pérez de. *A History of New Mexico*. Translated by Gilbert Espinosa. Los Angeles: The Quivira Society, 1933.

Waters, Frank. *Book of the Hopi*. New York: The Viking Press, 1963.

White, Leslie A. *The Pueblo of Sia, New Mexico*. Smithsonian Institution Bureau of American Ethnology, Bulletin 184. Washington: Government Printing Office, 1962.

Index